FLOWERS IN CHURCH

This book is dedicated to those who with love and patience spend time arranging flowers in churches and through their work make such a valuable contribution to the services of worship and to the beauty of the church.

'Angels' work is church decoration, work fit for angels that is. It is work immediately for the Glory of God, ...'

From the *Girls' Own Book*, 1876.

CONTENTS

FLOWERS IN CHURCH

Flowers are arranged in churches to make a more beautiful setting for the acts of worship. They bring life and colour to the church and are a continual reminder of the wonder of the natural world created by God. In this way they inspire worship.

Flowers also greet the visitor and provide a friendly atmosphere, making the church appear both cared for and a centre of happy activity.

Those who arrange flowers in church find that it is a most peaceful and satisfying occupation, but in order to create such beauty, in a simple and natural way, some knowledge is necessary. The most significant works of art are produced by artists who understand their materials, who are practised with their tools and techniques and who are knowledgeable about design. This book has been written for those who wish to know more and to stimulate ideas and provide helpful information about arranging flowers in church.

Flowers are admissible into our temples on all occasions as the fairest and most beautiful works of the Great Creator; they breathe only of purity, sweetness and truth – while they teach lessons of peace contentment and humility to us all.

F. W. BURBIDGE 1875

1

The First Time Flower Arranger

The first time you are invited to arrange flowers in a church you may, understandably, feel somewhat inadequate unless you are an experienced flower arranger. This makes some people reluctant to accept which is a pity because arranging church flowers is both enjoyable and rewarding. The procedure is easily found out, probably from the person who first asked you. No-one will expect a masterpiece the first time.

The Procedure

The following information is needed before you start:

The day and times when the flowers should be placed in the church.
The whereabouts of the key if the church is locked.
What should be done with any dead flowers from the previous week.
What should be done with any remaining fresh flowers.
Possible sources for flowers such as the gardens, shops, nurseries of church members.
Whether there is any cash allowance for flowers or if they are normally donated.
The whereabouts of containers, supports for stems, water and general equipment.
The position in which the flowers are to be placed.
If the flowers are to be removed after the Sunday evening service and, if so, their destination (sometimes they are taken to hospital or to sick or bereaved members of the congregation).

Obtaining Flowers and Leaves

Garden and nursery flowers should be picked the evening before or early in the morning of the day on which they are to be arranged. This is because they need a minimum of two hours, preferably overnight, in deep, tepid water in a cool, dimly-lit place. This is called *conditioning*. Cut off about half an inch of the stem ends as the flowers are placed in the water because this helps to remove a seal which sometimes forms while they have been out of water. Conditioning makes sure that the stems are well filled with water before being placed in church. (See Chapter 4 for further details.)

Shop flowers may be bought the same day, or the day before they are arranged, and conditioning is unnecessary as the stems will have been soaked in the shop. It is helpful to tell the florist that longlasting flowers are needed for a church arrangement.

Some leaves will be needed to fill up spaces so that fewer flowers are necessary. They also soften the appearance of bare stems. Florists sometimes sell foliage if none is available in gardens. Foliage, with the exception of grey leaves, should be submerged under water in a bowl or sink overnight, or for a minimum of two hours, before it is arranged.

Packing Plant Material

Leaves remain turgid (full of water) when placed inside a polythene bag. Flowers are better if put carefully into a cardboard box with a little tissue paper to support the flower heads (florists can often supply a flower box). The lid can be replaced, or a sheet of polythene put over the top, to keep the flowers moist. Alternatively a large sheet of paper can be wrapped around the flowers for protection from the wind or strong sunshine.

Equipment

Equipment for arranging flowers may be available in the church but if not you will need to take with you:

    scissors, flower scissors are better than household scissors and may be bought from florists and flower clubs;

Equipment for an arrangement

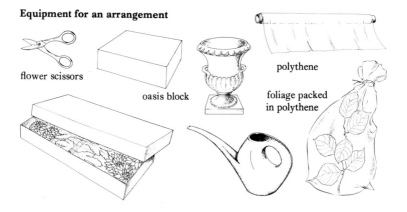

flower scissors

oasis block

polythene

foliage packed in polythene

polythene, a small sheet keeps the church surroundings clean as you
work;

a cardboard-box lid or a polythene bag for rubbish;

a small watering can with a long, thin spout for filling the container
(formerly called a vase);

support for the stems such as soaked foam (trade name Oasis,
Bloomfix and so on) or wire netting (see Chapter 2).

Containers are normally available in the church and if you are a
beginner it is advisable to choose an upright one, such as an urn. Boat-
shaped and shallow containers are more difficult to arrange at first.

Preparation

Clean the container.

Put in foam, or some loosely crumpled wire netting, securing it as
suggested on page 00.

Fill the container about one-third full of water.

Place the container in the position where it is to stand as this will give
you an idea of the height and shape for the eventual arrangement.

The sheet of polythene may be placed under or around the container
to keep the surroundings clean.

Make quite sure that the container cannot fall over easily.

You are now ready to begin arranging the flowers so let yourself go
and enjoy the pleasure of working with beautiful materials, provided by
nature.

Simple Guidelines

An uncomplicated round, or oval, massed style is the easiest for a
beginner. Place the tallest stems in the centre, remembering that the
flowers should look more important than the container and that one way
to do this is to make them taller than the height of the container. On the
other hand they do not want to be so tall that the arrangement becomes
top-heavy and topples over.

The flowers in the centre usually look better facing forward and the
flowers at the sides may face outwards which gives a pleasing three-
dimensional and rounded effect. The sides of flowers are often just as
beautiful as the fronts.

If varying lengths of stem are cut the flower heads will not crowd each
other and will be dispersed through the arrangement.

Leave spaces between the flowers so that the shape of each can be clearly seen. A few leaves can be added to soften the appearance of bare stems.

It is advisable to go to the middle, or back, of the church once or twice while you are arranging the flowers. In this way you will see how they will appear to the members of the congregation. You may find it necessary to change the position of some flowers, remembering however that the less flowers are handled the better.

When you are reasonably happy with the arrangement, clear up any debris; top up the container with water, making sure all stems are in water; remove the polythene and admire the result. Rubbish can be placed on the compost heap in the churchyard, in the dustbin, or taken home for disposal.

A simple arrangement of dahlias and beech leaves arranged by Margery Chapman in St Wilfrid's Parish Church, Mobberley

2

Supports for Flower Stems

Flowers may be placed in water in a container without any means of support for the stems but it is more satisfactory to hold them firmly, using the simple equipment that is available. How to support stems in a container is one of the most important things to learn about arranging flowers. They tend to crowd each other when not properly supported but, when each flower is seen clearly, fewer are needed and this saves money. They are also more likely to stay in place if accidentally knocked by an exuberant choirboy. It is essential that church flower arrangements are stable.

There are several simple methods of supporting stems and the collective term used by flower arrangers for supports is '*mechanics*'.

Wire netting, one-inch and two-inch mesh, stocked by ironmongers.
Plastic foam that takes up and retains water, obtainable from a flower shop or a flower club. It goes by several trade names such as Oasis, Bloomfix.
Pinholders that consist of a lead base containing sharp vertical pins on which stems can be impaled. Also available from flower shops and flower clubs.

Wire netting

Wire netting is the most convenient stem support for containers in churches because it is inexpensive and can be used many times. It is no great loss when unintentionally thrown away with the faded flowers, as can easily happen. Its disadvantage is that it does not hold the stems quite as accurately in position as plastic foam or a pinholder and the stems take a little longer to insert. This makes it slower to use. Wire netting is used in two ways:

1. Crumpled up in the cavity of the container, for which two-inch mesh is the most suitable because it is pliable.
2. As a 'cap' over foam for which the more rigid one-inch mesh is normally used (see under Plastic foam).

Wire netting is sold by the yard in several widths. It is helpful to have a roll in the church flower cuboard for the use of all flower arrangers.

There are rigid selvedges on the edges that should be cut off, using flower scissors or wire cutters. Plastic-covered wire netting is available in green and white but it is bulky.

PUTTING WIRE NETTING INTO A CONTAINER

METHOD 1. When using a container with a deep cavity, cut a length of mesh as wide as the container and about three times the depth of the cavity. Bend it into a U-shape and then squeeze the centre part together. Push the netting into the container leaving the cut ends well above the rim. These are useful to wind around long stems to hold them more firmly in position.

METHOD 2. Crumple a square of netting into a ball and place it into the container, lifting the centre into a dome above the rim. Experience will soon teach you how much netting to use for each container. If there is too much the result is a labyrinth of netting in which it is impossible to insert any stems, so take it out and cut some off. If too little is used there is no support for the stems which will not stay in place.

Wire netting

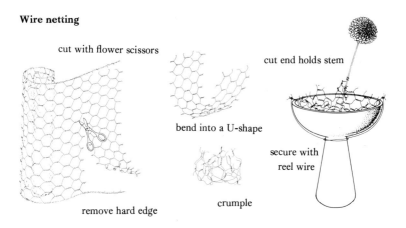

cut with flower scissors

cut end holds stem

bend into a U-shape

secure with reel wire

remove hard edge

crumple

HOLDING THE NETTING IN POSITION

The wire netting must be held down firmly. There are several ways of accomplishing this:

1. Tie up the container and netting together like a parcel, using green string or reel wire (from a florist or flower club). Plant material hides this when the arrangement is completed.
2. Hold the netting down with sticky tape in two directions remembering that it will not adhere to wet surfaces.

6

3. When using a container with a stem, twist the end of a length of reel wire on to one side of the netting, carry it once around the narrowest part of the stem and up on to the other side of the netting, to which you attach it, cutting off any surplus reel wire. This can be repeated at right angles for extra firmness.
4. When using a container with handles, the netting may be attached to the handles using string or wire. A second length of wire may be necessary in the opposite direction.
5. When using long, hard or woody stems, it is better to add a heavy pinholder for supporting the stem end. This should be placed in the bottom of the container's cavity and under the netting. The first stem is placed through the netting and pushed on to the pinholder. This holds the netting in place and no wire or string is necessary. Further stems may be inserted in the same way and others placed only into the netting.

Holding netting in position

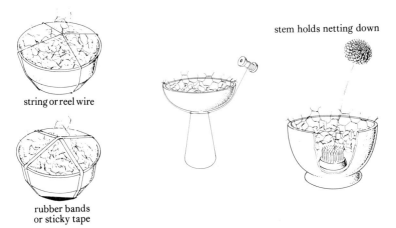

string or reel wire

rubber bands
or sticky tape

stem holds netting down

6. The netting in bowls can easily be held in position by placing a wide rubber band over both netting and container. A second band can be placed at right angles to it.

Plastic foam

Plastic foam is sold in a variety of shapes and sizes. One type absorbs and retains water; another type does not hold water and is intended for dried plant material. Make sure that you buy the correct kind. Every type of stem can take up water from plastic foam. However soft stems

7

are sometimes difficult to insert as they bend and so are better arranged in wire netting.

Foam is an accurate support as once a stem is pushed in firmly it will remain in position. For this reason it is quick to use. It is invaluable for containers which do not hold water but, when polythene lined, can hold foam. It is also useful for positions such as a sloping window sill where a container cannot stand. When arranging the flowers, stems can be placed into foam so that they flow downwards. This is not possible with a pinholder and more difficult with wire netting. It is more expensive to use than other supports because it cannot be used indefinitely. Each stem makes a permanent hole and eventually it has so many holes that it will neither support stems nor hold water. It is possible to use foam more than once but not if many flowers are used in an arrangement. A church flower committee may buy a box of foam for the flower cupboard, but if money is short individual flower arrangers may choose to use it at their own expense because it is easy.

PREPARATION

Foam, wet or dry, may be cut with a knife into different shapes and smaller blocks. To soak it before use, it should be placed in water *deeper* than itself; a washing-up bowl, deep bucket or kitchen sink is suitable.

Foam

foam blocks   soaking foam   stems can flow down

When the block of foam sinks level with the surface of the water it is ready to use. A 9-inch block takes about fifteen minutes and smaller blocks about five minutes. If foam is left in water for longer it cannot become too full. Foam is very light when dry and a block, 9 inches by 4 inches by 3 inches, weighs about 2 ounces. When full of water it weighs 4 pounds. This weight helps to stabilise the container.

PLACING FOAM IN CONTAINERS

DEEP CONTAINER. Cut a block to fit the cavity of the container but large enough to stick up above the rim for an inch or more depending on the

8

size of the container. This enables stems to be inserted to flow downwards. The high walls of the container hold the foam in position and no further equipment is necessary.

WIDE CONTAINERS. It is extravagant and unnecessary to fill a wide container with foam and it usually makes the design look too heavy at the base. A smaller container may be placed in the centre to hold the foam or fix a special pinholder with pins set wide apart to hold the block. A normal pinholder will become clogged up.

SHALLOW CONTAINERS. There is not enough support for the foam when a shallow container is used because the sides are too low. Extra

Securing foam

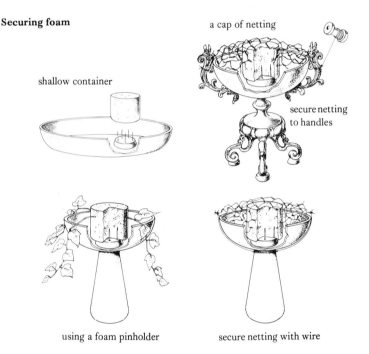

a cap of netting

shallow container

secure netting to handles

using a foam pinholder

secure netting with wire

support may be provided with a foam pinholder but I prefer to add a cap of one-inch wire netting to hold everything firmly in place. Cut a piece which will fit over the top of the foam and partly down the sides, like a cap, but do not crumple the netting as this cuts the foam. Secure the netting in place with reel wire or string for complete safety (see wire netting).

Thick woody stems are heavy and may slip in foam. A cap of wire netting held securely down prevents this as it provides a second support. People who are just starting flower arrangement are inclined to put stems in and out of foam and again the wire netting cap provides a 'fall back' support when the foam becomes full of holes.

AFTERCARE OF FOAM

The top surface of foam in an arrangement dries in a hot room or dry atmosphere. Smaller blocks can dry out completely so that the flowers wilt. To prevent this it is advisable to pour a little water now and again on to the top surface of the foam, being careful that it does not leak on to any table or furnishings. When not in use damp foam should be kept in a polythene bag because once dried out it is difficult to get it to take up water again. If by chance a block does dry out completely drop it into a pan of boiling water until it sinks down. This means it has taken up water again.

Pinholders

Pinholders are ideal for simple sparse arrangements and essential for designs which use heavy, woody stems. They do not hold very slim stems which slip between the pins. Smaller pinholders are unsuitable for

Pinholders

foam pinholder

foam pinholder

plasticine used
to secure

stems used
as mechanics

plasticine used
to secure

impaling a stem

church work as they hold only a few stems, lack weight and do not stay firmly in position in a container. Only the bigger ones, at least 3 inches in diameter, are recommended. These are heavy and not easily thrown away (unintentionally) with dead flowers. It is well worth buying good quality, rustless pinholders in the first place because, although expensive, they have longer pins, set more closely together, and are heavier than cheaper pinholders. A number of foam pinholders with wide-apart pins are useful to have in the church flower cupboard but flower arrangers should be reminded that it is easy to throw them away, by mistake, when discarding old foam.

Heavy pinholders stay in position very well in a container but when extra firmness is necessary, and in the case of the lighter foam pinholders, it is advisable to use plasticine. Special compounds are also obtainable and sealing strip is an alternative. All surfaces must be dry or the plasticine will not adhere. Roll it into a sausage or into several small blobs and stick them on to the underside of the pinholder. Place the pinholder on to the base of the container and press it down giving a twist as you do so.

Pinholders can become dirty and bits of plant material can clog up the pins but they can easily be cleaned with a strong wire brush. This is a dusty job which is better done out-of-doors.

Emergency mechanics

If no mechanics are available and it is essential to complete a flower arrangement, a tall, fairly narrow container can be filled with straight, preferably woody, stems which will hold flower stems in position reasonably well. Often there is a shrub in the churchyard that will provide a few lengths of woody stem. Fill the container and then cut the stems off just above the rim. If the flower stems seem squashed remove a few of the 'mechanic' stems.

It is also possible to fill a similar container with newspaper which acts as a support and sand or gravel will hold light stems. In all instances remember to fill the container with water.

Mechanics for altar vases

Many altar vases are copies of ones used centuries ago for perhaps one stem of Lilium candidum, the Madonna lily. I think they often look better arranged very simply with one lovely stem of flowers. The mechanics are not easy because most altar vases are tall and narrow. There are several ways of supporting flowers in them:

1. *Sand*, or fine gravel, may be poured into the vase to reach about two-thirds of the way up. This gives extra weight which is good for stability but it also means that a pinholder or a crumpled ball of

11

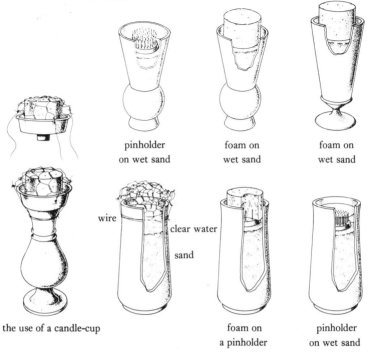

pinholder
on wet sand

foam on
wet sand

foam on
wet sand

wire

clear water

sand

the use of a candle-cup

foam on
a pinholder

pinholder
on wet sand

wire netting can be placed on top of it. Water should be poured on the sand until there is about 2 inches of clear water on top. Deep sand, without a pinholder or wire netting, will often support stems if they are not heavy.

2. *Foam* may drop down into the vase and be difficult to remove. It can rest on top of sand (or fine gravel) or alternatively a candle cup (see containers) can be secured with plasticine to the top of the vase. A block of foam capped by wire netting can be placed in the candlecup.

3. *Wire netting* may be used in a roll placed downwards in the container with some of it sticking well out of the container and fanning out. However when a vase has a narrow neck with a wider base the sand method is better.

An altar vase makes an excellent small pedestal and *with permission* it may be turned upside down and a container, such as a small pudding bowl, may be placed on top secured firmly with plasticine. This may be filled with foam or wire netting.

Spring flowers arranged by Doris Hunt using a candlecup in an altar vase. By courtesy of Farmers Weekly

13

When altar vases have unusually narrow necks it is easier to dispense with the usual mechanics and to arrange a simple bunch of flowers in the hand. Ask someone to tie it up with wool or string for you as you hold it and then drop the stems into the neck of the vase.

Mechanics for Altar vases

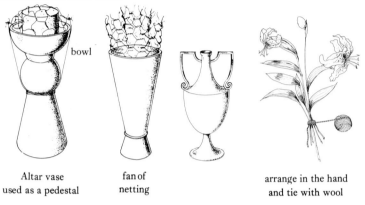

| Altar vase used as a pedestal | fan of netting | | arrange in the hand and tie with wool |

Mechanics for tall branches

Long arching, branches of fruit blossom, forsythia, lime, catkins, escallonia and so on, can look especially beautiful but they are not easy to support in a container. It is well worth having some lengths of galvanised piping welded together by a metal worker for placing towards the centre back of a large container. Each pipe should be at least 5 inches in height to give good support and a variety of heights, with the taller pipe towards the back is practical. One heavy branch may be placed into each pipe. Wire netting or foam can surround this central grouping for other shorter stemmed flowers. If a group of pipes is made to fit your church containers do experiment with their height first.

Adding height to a container

Often long-stemmed flowers are not available and yet would improve the look of a bowl of flowers. Metal cones may be bought at florists and flower clubs and these hold water and a few stems of flowers. Tape, using any type of sticky tape, one or more cones (sometimes called tubes) to a long stick. Sticks in the form of dowelling can be bought at DIY shops in many lengths and widths, but square ones are best. Alternatively a garden centre may be able to provide thin stakes normally used for houseplants. The stick should be a few inches taller than the top

Adding height

stick

metal tube

sticky tape

welded piping

cone

sticky tape · cone for water ·

stick

cone because then the top stems of flowers can be wired to it for support. *Before* starting the arrangement, place the stick through the wire netting or foam in the container and on to a pinholder if used. Remember to fill every cone with water. Make sure the stick of cones is safe and it may be necessary to squeeze the wire netting around the stick. First place the flowers in the cones which can be hidden by plant material placed lower down in the arrangement. Cones on sticks are often used in pedestal arrangements to give extra height. They may be filled with foam or wire netting.

Wiring stems

Wiring can make naturally graceful stems too rigid in appearance but now and again it is necessary to support a floppy stem, or to provide a false stem for such plant material as pine cones. Stub wires from florists and flower clubs are short, strong lengths of wire, in varying lengths and

15

gauges. The finer the wire the higher numbered the gauge. Numbers 20 and 22 are useful.

PINE CONES. Place a stub wire either side of the central core, tucking it into the scales so that the two wires are parallel. Twist them together on either side of the cone, bend them down below the cone and then twist

Wiring a pine cone

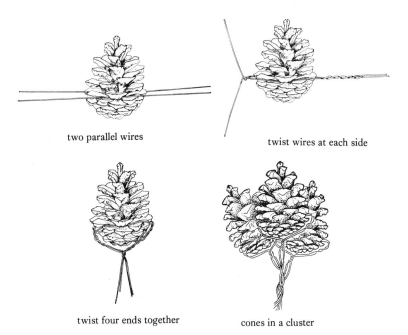

two parallel wires

twist wires at each side

twist four ends together

cones in a cluster

all four ends together. The wires are now easily placed into foam or can be attached to a short stick. Several cones may be clustered together in a spray.

HEAVY FLOWER HEADS AND BROKEN STEMS. Flowers such as hyacinth can be too heavy for their own stems. Run a strong wire gently inside the stem and cut it off about 2 inches below the stem end. When the flower is placed into an arrangement the wire will support it in the mechanics but do make sure the stem end is in water. Bent or broken stems may be wired in the same way.

FLOPPY STEMS. Tulip stems seem to go just where they please however they are arranged at first. To prevent this pierce the stem close to the flower head with a wire at least as long as the stem. Turn down $\frac{1}{4}$-inch of the wire so that it will not pull out. Twist the remainder down the stem in big twists and place flower stem and wire together into the mechanics.

Wiring

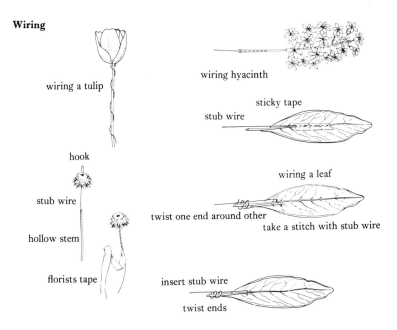

wiring a tulip

wiring hyacinth

sticky tape

stub wire

hook

wiring a leaf

stub wire

twist one end around other

take a stitch with stub wire

hollow stem

florists tape

insert stub wire

twist ends

LEAVES. Preserved and dried leaves that are so useful during the winter months often need a false stem. There are several methods of doing this.

1. Place a long stub wire on the back of a leaf in the centre and alongside any short stem which may be still attached. Place some sticky tape over the wire and on to the leaf to hold it in position. Twist the wire around the remaining leaf stem.
2. Make a stitch with fine wire across the leaf about a third of the way up from where it joins the leaf stem. Turn down the ends of the wire and twist them around each other catching in any remaining leaf stem.
3. Push a wire from front to back through the centre of a leaf and about half an inch above the stem and leaf joint. Bend the wire down on both sides of the leaf and wind one around the other catching in any remaining leaf stem.

DRIED FLOWERS. The stems of many dried flowers shrivel and may be given a false stem of wire. This is better done before the flowers dry as it

17

is then difficult to get the wire through the dried tissue. After harvesting the flowers, such as annual everlastings, cut off the fresh stem and push a stubwire through the centre of the flower, gradually drawing it down until it disappears. The flower will tighten on to the wire as it dries. For extra safety the wire may be turned over in a tiny hook at the top. This is then pulled down into the centre of the flower as before. To hide the stem it may be bound with florists' tape or inserted into the hollow stem of some other plant such as a grass.

Dowel

A bundle of lengths of dowel from a DIY shop is a useful addition to the church flower cupboard. They can be used to lengthen stems of dried plant material and also for supporting fruit in an arrangement.

Other supports

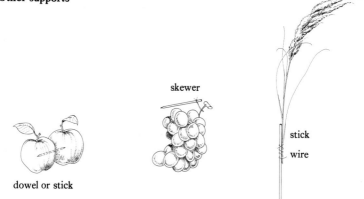

skewer

stick

wire

dowel or stick

SUPPORTING FRUIT. Push the fruit such as an apple or orange well on to whatever length of dowel you want for the arrangement and place the other end into the wire netting or foam in the container. When fruit is used at such times as harvest festivals, short lengths of dowel pushed into one fruit and then into another will stop them from rolling about. Grapes can be supported by wiring a bunch to a length of dowel, placed into the mechanics.

LENGTHENING STEMS. Place a length of dowel alongside a dried stem for about 4 inches. (This method is no use for lengthening stems of fresh plant material because their ends must be in water.) Twist a stub wire around the dowel and stem together. Cut the dowel to whatever length you want for the arrangement.

18

3

Containers and Vases

Vases for holding water and the stems of flowers and leaves are now called *containers* by flower arrangers. Altar vases used on the Communion table are an exception. Containers may be visible, as part of the arrangement, or be concealed by flowers and leaves and act merely as a receptacle for holding water and stems. When the container can be seen it should be attractive and also suit the flowers. Concealed containers need not be decorative and such things as baking tins may be used.

It is well worthwhile choosing a container to match the flowers and leaves for an arrangement. Each part of a design contributes to the final effect and if the parts do not match the whole appearance is less attractive. Both size and colour are important. For example, large hydrangea heads look top heavy in a small container and blue flowers are unlikely to blend well with a brilliant scarlet container.

Colour

Colour is the most important consideration because it attracts our eyes immediately. Some colours blend more easily than others with the colours of flowers and leaves and are therefore better for containers. Those with brilliant colouring outshine the flowers, especially if the surface is very highly glazed and shiny. White can also be difficult as it is very eye-attracting although it can look lovely with white or pastel-coloured flowers. If for example red flowers are arranged in a white container the flowers and the container appear as two separated and uncoordinated parts. If there are several white containers in the church flower cupboard some could be painted a different colour. There are two ways of harmonising the container and the plant material in an arrangement:

1. Use one of the 'earthy' colours for the container. Browns, greys, dull greens, beiges, the colours of stone and metal all blend easily with plant material of any colour.
2. Use the colour of the container in some or all of the flowers and leaves; yellow flowers look attractive in a brass container, white daisies in white pottery, rust-coloured chrysanthemums in a terracotta or brown container. Some colour link is very helpful. If you have some long stems of delphiniums in a wonderful shade of blue

and the only suitably sized container is an orange one, link the two colours by using some bronze foliage such as copper beech (or green beech preserved with glycerine) with the flowers.

Stone-coloured containers are especially suitable for a church as they blend well with the walls and metal always looks pleasing and suitable. Yellow, cream and green are good with brass; white, grey, pink and other pastel colours with silver; blues, mauves, pinks, violets and red with pewter; apricot, red, orange, peach, pink, browns with copper; any colour goes with bronze, iron and stone.

Unfortunately metal containers are expensive and not easy to find these days but there are handmade, stoneware containers that are available in excellent colours for flowers. There is also a large range of modern, mass-produced pottery in earthy colours, including baking dishes and stew pots that can be used for flowers as well as for cooking.

CHANGING THE COLOUR. If the colour of a container is unsuitable but the shape and size are correct one or two coats of paint will help. A stone-coloured mat paint, such as an emulsion, is ideal and there is a mat, black-board paint in an excellent green. It is advisable to rub with sandpaper a shiny-surfaced container. This scratches it slightly and helps the paint to adhere. Handfuls of sand added to the tin of wet paint gives a rough texture that is attractive. Glossy paint is too dominant for flowers.

An inexpensive white plastic urn

The same urn painted to resemble stone

Shape

Urns are the most useful shape for church arrangements and are easy to use. They hold plenty of water and do not need topping up often.

They are normally heavy and their large base makes them stable.

They may be used with foam or with wire netting. Stone garden urns are ideal and, although heavy, they can be left permanently in position and blend beautifully with stone walls. White, plastic urns are inexpensive and may be bought at chain stores. Although the colour and texture are unsuitable, the shape is similar to old garden urns. After sandpapering the plastic surface, paint it with stone-coloured emulsion paint containing some sand. The final effect can be similar to a real stone urn.

Garden urns normally have a hole in the bottom as they are intended for outdoor plants that need drainage. A plastic bowl, a tin or polythene can be used as a liner, or the hole can be stopped up with a plug, cork, plasticine or sealing compound. Some urns have a large cavity and to avoid the necessity for long stems or a large quantity of foam it is better to put a smaller container inside the urn to hold the mechanics. Plant saucers and plant pots without holes in the bottom, plastic bowls and baking tins may be used as an inner liner. They can be made quite secure with plasticine or a similar compound pressed on to the bottom.

Containers with stems are always attractive as they lift up the flower arrangement giving space below the design. This means that the lower flowers can be seen easily, and graceful, curving stems can be used to flow downwards.

Shallow containers have very limited use in a church and so do containers that hold little water. When water is limited because of the size of the container the flowers soon fade. It is not practical with church flower arrangements to top up the container daily.

Size

Containers used in churches and certainly in cathedrals should normally be bigger than those used in the average home. Height is also needed so that the arrangement is in proportion with the lofty roof and a large container is necessary for visual balance.

The Church container collection

Many containers are given to the church but it is important that an experienced person should give advice to people wishing to donate them. Many containers are unsuitable and can be difficult to use, putting people off doing the flowers. They can also be unsuitable for the church itself. The architect for a new church may design the flower containers and this is ideal as they normally blend beautifully. However, there should be some consultation between the architect and the flower arrangers with regard to size, shape and intended position.

A church's collection of containers often grows in a haphazard

21

manner over the years and it is really better for the flower committee to discard those that are never used. A coffee morning or a bring-and-buy or plant sale could provide the funds for a few specially purchased containers of good quality and suitable in shape and colour. It is helpful to decide the positions in the church that are normally used for flowers and then to buy containers for each situation.

A useful church flower arrangement container should:

Be large enough to hold plenty of water or foam.
Be fairly heavy with a broad base so that it cannot fall over easily.
Have a round cavity, rather than a boat-shaped one which is harder to use.
Suit the intended setting.
Be a suitable colour for most plant material.

THE SETTING

Containers that can be seen by the congregation should be suitable for the setting. Simple, classical shapes are good in any surroundings. Traditional churches should have traditional containers but more modern churches can have a simple modern style. It is also important to consider the size and colour of the container in its intended setting so that the two are harmonious.

IDEAS

Containers can be found in antique shops, market stalls, bazaars, garden

Suitable containers

22

centres, flower shops, second-hand shops, auction sales, craft shops, potteries, kitchen shops. Some suitable containers are:

    garden urns in stone, fibreglass, asbestos, plastic;
    large bowls and basins in pottery, bulb bowls;
    modern, handmade stoneware;
    large baking dishes, vegetable and soup tureens;
    jardinières, troughs;
    Victorian wash-bowls;
    large jugs and pitchers, brass and copper pans and jam pans;
    coal and log holders in metal;
    egg and bread crocks in earthenware;
    antique metal tea urns and wine coolers;

Containers that are not watertight can be used if lined with polythene, a baking tin, plant saucer or bowl, and include:

    baskets and trugs of all types;
    wooden chests and boxes;
    small garden wheel barrows, tubs;

Suitable containers

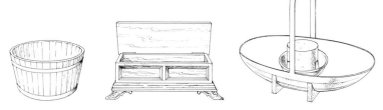

    tea-caddies, salt boxes, bible boxes;
    bicycle baskets for walls;
    small occasional tables.

HOME-MADE CONTAINERS

It is possible to make, or contrive, containers for use in a church but it is important that the end result is of good quality and well finished. Suggestions:

1. Hand-made pottery (a group could attend a pottery class).
2. A drain pipe, especially the creamy coloured variety with a mottled texture, that can be used as a pedestal in a modern church, with a baking tin on the top to hold the mechanics.

A five feet high design of driftwood, hosta leaves and white agapanthus in a hand-made stoneware container

3. A single pillar from a fourposter bed, or a baluster from a staircase, for use as a pedestal, with the addition of a base and a small shelf at the top for a container.
4. An inexpensive, plastic urn glued to a block of wood, the two painted in the same colour.
5. An upturned meat-dish cover placed on an iron stand made at a forge.

6. A trivet with a baking dish on top.
7. Sheet lead knocked up into a container, using a small block of wood and a hammer.
8. A large round cake tin daubed with Snowcem, roughened to give a pleasing texture, and painted.

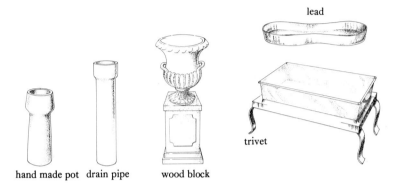

lead

trivet

hand made pot   drain pipe   wood block

CONCEALED CONTAINERS

Anything that holds water can be used as a container if it is concealed by plant material or placed inside a decorative container.

    1. Watertight *baking tins* in various sizes and shapes, loaf and cake tins, pudding bowls, empty paint cans and buckets are all useful. They may be used inside baskets and other containers that are

Containers for concealing

   bread tin   cake tin   foam saucer

    decorative but do not hold water. They can be placed on top of pedestals and covered by foliage and flowers. They can be used on top of rood screens or on the floor. It is best to paint tin with emulsion paint in black, dark green, brown or dark grey, so that it does not shine through the plant material.

    2. For smaller arrangements inexpensive *plastic saucers* obtainable from flower shops and flower clubs are made especially for blocks of foam. These are easily concealed by the plant material used.

When the flowers are taken to ill or bereaved people after the Sunday services, they can be carried already arranged in the foam and saucer.

3. *Candlecups,* obtainable from florists and flower clubs, can be useful when placed into a narrow-necked container such as a candlestick, or a bottle with a narrow neck. They can also be used in the top of altar vases. The mechanics are the same as for other containers. As they hold little water, only a few flowers should be arranged in them. They must be topped up every few days and if foam is used this must be watered often.

4. *Tubes or cones* are useful containers for one or two flowers. They hold water, foam or wire netting and are normally used for stems that need to be given height, or for placing flowers high up in a

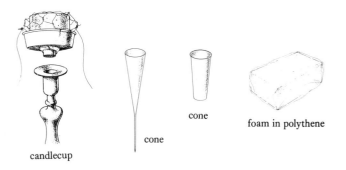

candlecup

cone

cone

foam in polythene

design for a special effect. Tubes made for the purpose are sold by florists. Discarded cigar holders, orchid tubes and test tubes are useful for one or two flowers or leaves. They should be attached to a cane of the required length with sticky tape. A square cane such as a dahlia stick, or the stick used by growers in packing flowers, is the easiest to use. The cone does not slip as it may when a round cane or stick is used. DIY shops and garden centres sell canes. All canes should be concealed by arranging plant material in front of them.

5. *A thin polythene bag,* containing a block of foam, makes an excellent concealed container and can be used for awkward places such as sloping windowsills. It should be wrapped in wire netting and wired with reel wire to the window frame. A similar bag of foam can also be suspended from a ceiling light bracket or wall, or used on a pulpit or lectern. The polythene holds in the water, but do not place stems through the bottom of the bag where water may

gather as it will drip out if there are holes. If the wire netting is placed next to the foam and *inside* the polythene, surfaces will not be scratched. Make a hole in the polythene and place real wire through it. Twist it on to the netting. This enables the 'container' to be hung up or wired into a certain position. Cut away surplus polythene after the bag has been tied up tightly. Woody and hard stems will go easily through the polythene but a hole for softer stems may have to be made with a skewer.

CLEANING AND REPAIRING CONTAINERS

From time to time it is necessary to give the church containers a good clean. This removes dirt that causes bacteria and shortens the life of flowers.

GLASS. Wash with warm soapy water every time the container is used. A piece of lemon dipped in salt or a little Milton or vinegar is helpful. Polish glass occasionally with methylated spirit. Badly stained glass usually responds to soaking and brushing with a soft brush. Inaccessible interiors may be cleaned by gently pouring in coarse sand or rice with warm, soapy water and swirling the mixture around.

ALABASTER. No water should be used in an alabaster container without an inner lining of polythene (or a hidden container). Alternatively swill melted candle wax around the inside of the cavity to seal the alabaster. Clean with salad oil rather than water.

SILVER. Clean with silver polish but to avoid scratching with wire netting line the container with thin polythene, or a hidden container. Store silver in a polythene bag to lessen tarnishing.

COPPER, BRASS. Clean with metal polish, preferably the long-term solution. If a permanent seal of lacquer is applied it should be done by a professional. This eliminates all cleaning but can change the mellow appearance a little. When not lacquered use lemon, or vinegar and salt, to remove stubborn stains. Rinse well and then polish with metal polish. Silicone wax used for polishing cars protects the surface from tarnish for a few weeks. Store the containers in polythene bags to lessen tarnishing.

IRON. Paraffin oil softens rust and helps to clean iron containers.

MARBLE. Use soap flakes dissolved in warm water and a soft brush.

Pedestals

Pedestals of varying heights are invaluable for use in a church as they lift the flower arrangement up. Adjustable wrought iron and fibreglass

Pedestals

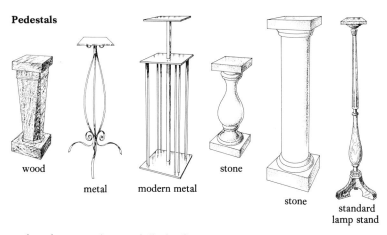

wood

metal

modern metal

stone

stone

standard
lamp stand

pedestals are made especially for flowers and the latter can be finished to look like stone. Alabaster, marble and wooden pedestals are sometimes available. Old lamp standards can be converted into flower arrangement pedestals if a shelf is placed on the top of the electrical fittings. A stone mason may be able to make a simple column for use as a pedestal. Its weight and colour make stone especially suitable in a church with stone walls.

The mechanics for a pedestal arrangement, as it is called, are not difficult. Place a painted cake tin or a large black bowl on the top of the pedestal. Put one or more blocks of foam in the bowl to stand well out of the container. (This is so that stems can be inserted to flow downwards.) Place one-inch-mesh wire netting over the foam and pull it up above it in a mound to give extra support for the long stems. Fix a length of real wire to one side of the wire netting and carry it around the stem of the pedestal and up to the other side of the container where it should be twisted on to the wire netting. Repeat at right angles with another length of reel wire. String can be used similarly but is more obvious. It may be necessary to wire a very tall pedestal to a built-in part of the church such as a screen, column or pew end, using reel wire. This makes it impossible to knock the pedestal over. Two-inch-mesh wire netting can be crumpled into a large ball if no foam is available. Wire it on to the container and pedestal as described. It is not as easy to use as foam and it is helpful to place a large pinholder in the bottom of the container on which to impale the central stems.

28

Bases

Bases, plinths and stands of various types can be used to raise flower arrangements up so that they can be better seen. They may also be used to protect table-tops. They are not usually necessary if the container has a built-in base.

Bases

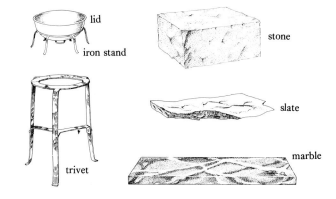

lid

iron stand

stone

slate

trivet

marble

It is important that any type of base suits the church, the container and the plant material. Large blocks of stone can look harmonious in an old church with stone walls. Marble bases may also be suitable and sometimes the tops of old washstands can be found. Stone masons can cut marble and stone to a required shape and size, but bases of these materials may be expensive. In a country village church old roof slates may be suitable. Local materials, and materials similar to the fabric of the church, always blend in well with the surroundings but fabric covered boards and mats are not normally harmonious. Metal workers can often weld iron into useful stands and these may be made especially to fit certain containers. Simplicity is advisable as complicated designs detract from the flowers.

4

Longlasting Flowers

Flowers arranged in a church should always look fresh, both for Sunday services and for the visitors who may drop by during the week. For reasons of economy and time it is not usual to renew flowers during the week. It is therefore essential to do everything that is possible to make them last well. Few things look more depressing or give a more uncared-for appearance than a vase of drooping, faded flowers. Some churches are locked during the week and the flowers are often sent to a sick member of the congregation. In this event it is also desirable to have flowers which are in good condition.

The life-span of flowers varies according to the type of flower and it is sensible to buy or pick those which normally live a long time. A few buds, as well as the more open flowers, should be included in the arrangement because these will gradually open out and look fresh later in the week. They also provide an interesting variety of size.

Although other factors, such as heat, draughts, dry atmosphere, and lack of water contribute to the length of a flower's life, the following normally last especially well:

Acanthus	Dahlia	Orchid
Achillea	Delphinium	Pyrethrum
Allium	Eryngium	Rose (some varieties)
Alstroemaria	Freesia	Scabious
Amaryllis	Gladiolus	Strelitzia
Anthurium	Grasses	Sweet William
Antirrhinum	Hyacinth	Straw flower and other
Aster	Hydrangea	annuals which dry
Carnation	(late Summer)	Tulip
Chrysanthemum	Lily	
Clivia	Marguerite	

Foliage

Many leaves last longer than flowers and may be used for several weeks. Evergreen foliage keeps well and there are many hardy perennials with useful leaves (see Chapter 7). Young foliage, however, wilts quickly because the protective, outer covering has not developed sufficiently and water is rapidly lost from the leaf surface. After May hardy perennial foliage is more reliable and in the middle and late summer it lasts very well. All very thin-tissued leaves, such as those of wild flowers, flop almost at once and there is some foliage which cannot be made to stand up at all after it is cut.

Florists' flowers

If it is necessary to buy flowers for the church, Thursday, Friday and Saturday are good days. Florists are very helpful about recommending longlasting, fresh flowers and there are signs to look for which indicate young flowers and leaves:

Light yellow centres in daisy-type flowers, older flowers have darker yellow centres.
Buds, especially of spring flowers, as these open quickly.
Tightly curled petals in the centre of chrysanthemums.
Tulips with crisp, squeaky leaves.
Stems which are green, unmarked and not slimy.
Leaves which are crisp and bright, not dry or brown.
Tight centres and no floppy outside petals on carnations.
Scabious with greenish centres.
Gladioli with only one or two open florets low down on the stem.
Arum lilies with light yellow centres.
Lilies which are just opening with firm and not crêpey petals.

Flowers bought from a flower shop will have been prepared and are ready for immediate use. They should be placed in a bucket of tepid water until taken to the church. When placing them in an arrangement cut off about half an inch of stem because when out of water this may have started to harden, stopping the absorption of water.

Garden and nursery flowers

Many garden flowers are not as longlasting as those sold by florists which have been chosen by the trade for their lasting properties. However, with a little care in preparation, garden flowers are very successful and economical. They also have their own simple charm and beauty.

The best time for picking garden flowers is in the evening as the stems can then be soaked in water overnight and the flowers are full of water and ready for arranging next day. If picked in the morning of the day on which they are to be arranged the stems should first be given at least two hours in deep water. Pick buds showing colour and half-open flowers rather than mature, open ones. Cut the stems on a slant to

31

provide a greater surface for absorbing water. Place in water immediately.

Preparation of garden plant material

A little care taken over the preparation of garden flowers and leaves before arranging them makes a tremendous difference to their powers of lasting. When flowers and leaves are cut from a plant their source of water is lost and another must be provided or the cutting wilts. Replacing the source of water, by means of a container holding plenty of water, is easy. This is, however, only half the story as some stem-ends do not take it up unless they are specially prepared by the flower arranger. The treatment varies and is determined by the structure of the stem tissue.

ALL STEMS

Cut off about half an inch from all stem ends. This removes any hard callus which may have formed while the stem has been away from water, and also removes any airlock which can prevent water from rising up the stem. Cuts are better made on a slant to give a greater surface area for absorption of water. After this first preparation of stems treat them according to type as follows:

WOODY STEMS. Scrape the bark away from the outside of about 2 inches of stem, using a small knife or a potato peeler. (Bark is a protective outer covering which prevents water from entering.) Then expose

Preparation of plant material

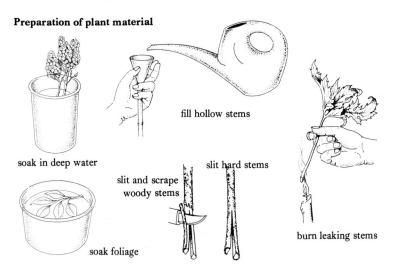

fill hollow stems

soak in deep water

slit and scrape
woody stems

slit hard stems

soak foliage

burn leaking stems

more of the inner softer tissue by cutting upwards in to the stem with flower scissors for about 1 to 2 inches. More than one cut may be made in thicker stems. Forsythia and cherry are examples of plants with woody stems.

HARD STEMS. No scraping is necessary but it is advisable to cut up into the stem in the same way as for woody stems. Roses and chrysanthemums are examples of plants with hard stems.

HOLLOW STEMS. There are not many plants with hollow stems but the popular delphiniums, lupins and some dahlia stems are examples. These may be filled by turning the stem upside down and pouring in water by means of a thin spouted watering can or a small funnel. The end of the stem should be plugged with cotton wool which also acts as a wick, drawing more water into the stem when it is placed in a bucket of water.

SOFT STEMS. Many plants such as spring bulbous flowers and some hardy perennials have soft stems and they take in water easily. No further preparation is necessary beyond the initial snipping of the stem end.

LEAKING STEMS. A few stems such as poppies and the Christmas flower, poinsettia, have stems that leak a milky substance called latex that, when dry, can form a hard layer that prevents the uptake of water. The leaking stops if the stem end is held in the flame of a match or gas jet until sizzling stops. However, each time the stem is cut it should be charred again.

When the stem ends have been prepared place them immediately in deep, tepid water to soak, submerging as much as possible of the stem but not the flower itself as water may damage the petals. Flower buckets which are taller than the normal household bucket and have two side handles are available for this purpose from a florist or flower club. Leave the bucket in a cool, dimly lit place for at least two hours and preferably overnight. In this way the stems have plenty of time to take up water and the cool, dim position reduces transpiration (loss of water) from the petals and leaves. After this treatment the flowers should look fresh and lovely and be all set for a long life in an arrangement.

FOLIAGE

Leaves may be put to soak in the same bucket as the flowers and pushed under the water as this does no damage except to grey leaves. Their numerous small hairs become waterlogged, lose their grey appearance and drip water onto furniture. Treat grey foliage as for flowers.

When preparing (or conditioning) a larger quantity of foliage use a sink, or a bath if necessary, and after the normal stem treatment, push the leaves under the water for about two hours or overnight. No damage occurs and the leaves cannot lose any of the moisture that they already contain. This treatment ensures that they are full of water and firm before they are placed in an arrangement.

Water temperature

Tepid water travels more quickly up a stem than cold water and so it is advisable to use this for conditioning stems. Cold water is quite satisfactory for stems already prepared and soaked.

Hot water can be useful for stem ends when you wish to encourage tightly closed buds to open. It is also useful for wilted flowers as it travels quickly up the stem and revives the flower.

Boiling water has several uses; it sterilises the cut end of the stem and reduces micro-organisms that are present and produce slime to block

bag

The use of boiling water

the water channels in the stem; it prevents nutrients from leaking out as it kills the cells in the stem end; it prevents a callus forming (but this is easily removed by snipping off with flower scissors); it can help to remove air in the stem, which may stop the uptake of water, because the heat of the water makes the air expand and forces most of it out in a bubble.

Many flower arrangers like 'the boiling water treatment' for garden plant material. This method consists of holding one inch of the stem end in boiling water for about a minute and then putting it straight into deep tepid water. Alternatively, take the pan off the stove and let the water cool with the stem end in it. Whenever this method is used the flower head should be protected from the hot steam, which may damage delicate petals, with a polythene or paper bag.

34

CLEANING AND GROOMING. Foliage grown in towns and cities is often dusty or dirty. It is easily cleaned by swishing it in a sink of tepid water containing a little detergent. The more stubborn dirt may be wiped off with a wet, soapy tissue or cloth.

Damaged leaves should be cut away and those with frayed edges can be trimmed safely with flower scissors. Leaves under water in a container can become decayed and cause slime which shortens the flowers' lives, so any such leaves should be removed.

WATER IN THE CONTAINER

A deep container which holds a lot of water is essential for a church flower arrangement. This should contain enough water to supply the stem ends all week. The more flowers in the arrangement, the more water is necessary and an arrangement containing many flowers may need topping up during the week even if a deep container is used.

ADDITIVES TO THE WATER. There are many old wives' tales about water additives for making flowers last longer, but there is no substitute for good conditioning in the first place. A quarter of a teaspoon of a mild disinfectant such as Hibitane added to about a pint of water, especially in the case of longlasting chrysanthemums, is helpful as it discourages the formation of bacteria and, consequently, unpleasant smelling water and slime.

After care

The position in which the arrangement stands when completed makes a tremendous difference to the life of the flowers. If it is placed in a draught; in strong sunshine; near a hot radiator; in a very dry atmosphere, the most carefully conditioned and beautiful plant material can wilt overnight. A cool, dim, damp atmosphere is the best. Churches are normally cooler and darker than the average home, so the arrangement is off to a good start. However even these excellent conditions can be improved by spraying a mist of water around them.

A flower sprayer which produces a very fine spray of water is obtainable from florists and flower clubs and could be included in the church flower-arrangement cupboard. This makes it easy to spray the flowers immediately after they are arranged and if possible during the week as well.

The value of spraying is underestimated. Flower petals and leaves lose water as vapour all the time they are in a dry atmosphere (just as washing dries on a line). This is called *transpiration.* In a damp atmosphere flowers will not lose as much water. An occasional misting will provide a damp mini-atmosphere around the flowers and prevent wilting. This is especially helpful in winter when the damp outside air is excluded by closed doors and windows and the heating is turned on, often making the air a lot drier than in summer.

Wilted flowers

Wilted means dehydrated (lacking water) but not necessarily dead. Few flowers wilt if they have been well conditioned. Removing a wilted

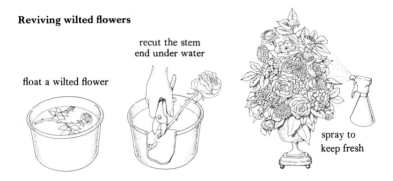

Reviving wilted flowers

recut the stem end under water

float a wilted flower

spray to keep fresh

flower from the arrangement may disturb the other flowers and upset the design and so it is usually better to cut the stem.

If you wish to revive a wilted flower there are several methods of persuading it to take up water again:

1. Float the entire flower and stem in tepid water, for about two hours. This is one of the better methods, especially for roses. Recut the stem end before replacing in the arrangement.
2. Recut the stem end under water to remove a possible callus and then stand the whole stem in deep, warm water for a few hours.
3. Recut the stem end and place it in an inch of boiling water. Remove the pan from the stove and allow the water to cool, leaving the stem in it.
4. Recut the stem end, place the stem in deep, warm water and spray the flower with a mister.

Forcing flowers

Forcing means bringing flowers into bloom earlier than normal. It is used for branches of spring blossom such as cherry, lilac and forsythia. The branches should be cut when large buds appear. Give the boiling water treatment and then place the branches in warm water in a sunny window.

Retarding flowers

It is helpful sometimes to be able to hold back the development of flowers, especially if they are wanted for a later day in the week. It is also useful to be able to bring some buds out into flower and hold others back when a bunch of flowers all at one stage of maturity is purchased. Flowers may be successfully retarded by being placed in a refrigerator. Condition them in the normal way and then put the flowers into a polythene bag and tie it up. Place the bag in the lower part of the refrigerator (the freezing compartment will destroy them). The flowers may be kept in this way for several days. For shorter periods they may be placed in a jug of water in the refrigerator. This method is more suitable for flowers with strong stems such as roses, chrysanthemums and tulips. Other flowers from the same bunch may be put in a warm room to bring them out so that buds, half-open and open flowers are obtained.

Special treatment

Most plant material should be prepared according to the type of stem tissue but a few plants, sometimes used in church arrangements, need different or extra treatment.

Allium	hot water should be avoided as the onion smell is exaggerated;
Aster	remove foliage from the stem;
Bells-of-Ireland	defoliate;
Berries	hair lacquer or clear varnish spray retards shrivelling;
Bulbous flowers	remove the white part of the stem; shallow water is better in the container;
Bulrush	spray with hair lacquer or clear varnish;
Chincherinchee	cut off the waxed ends used in transporting;
Gerbera	the boiling water treatment is essential;
Gladiolus	can be retarded in the bud stage if left out of water in a cool place;
Hippeastrum	fill the hollow stem with water after placing a long thin stick into it which will protrude slightly below the stem end; this supports the stem;
Holly	spray well as it soon dries out; the berries may be picked several weeks before Christmas to save them

	from the birds. Place the stems in a bucket half full of water and cover with a polythene bag tucked into the bucket; leave in a cool place until wanted;
Hydrangea	do not use when young as it easily wilts; if this happens spray well or submerge the flower head in water, but once wilted it is not easy to revive;
Ivy	spray well;
Kale	hot water increases the cabbage smell;
Lilac	remove the foliage from the stem;
Lily	remove the anthers with flower scissors as they stain fabric badly;
Pampas grass	spray with lacquer or varnish;
Peony	may be retarded in bud without water in a cool place;
Philadelphus	remove the leaves;
Poinsettia	charring the stem end is essential;
Poppy	charring the stem end is essential;
Strelitzia	the flowers may be gently eased from the sheath which contains more than one flower;
Sweet pea	handle carefully as damage is easily caused;
Tulip	condition rolled up in newspapers to give a straight stem;
Zinnia	a wire pushed into the flower head through the hollow stem keeps it upright;

Some flowers are very difficult to condition for long life and are not advised for normal church work. These include azaleas, camellias, clematis, coleus foliage, gardenias, hibiscus, laburnum, mimosa, pelargoniums, many wild flowers and some maples.

> *Loveliest of lovely things are they*
> *On earth that soonest pass away,*
> *The rose that lives a little hour*
> *Is prized beyond the sculptured flower.*

W.C. BRYANT

5

Arranging Church Flowers

Bright gems of earth, by which perchance we see
What Eden was – what paradise may be

UNKNOWN AUTHOR

Anyone who has arranged flowers in a church will agree that it is usually a special experience. In the quiet and serene atmosphere one feels close to God. Even when a festival is in preparation and the church is humming with people there is still a tranquil atmosphere.

Flower arranging in a church is different from flower arranging at home in several ways.

1. The space is much larger so arrangements need to be bigger. This means *larger* flowers and leaves and *longer* stems than you would use at home, rather than just more plant material.
2. The flowers need to be placed higher than usual so that they can be seen above the heads of people, whether standing or seated.
3. The colours of the flowers should be brighter or more luminous because they are seen from a greater distance in dimmer light. The windows in a church are often relatively small, stained glass reduces the light, and electric lighting is often weaker than at home.

General principles

SIZE

When you make a miniature arrangement, for a container the size of a thimble, you choose tiny flowers and leaves. For the larger spaces in a church, bigger containers, leaves and flowers are needed, such as open roses and tulips, dahlias, rhododendrons, chrysanthemums, tall delphiniums, long branches of blossom and foliage.

FORM

Bold and distinctive forms are more easily seen from a distance and lilies, and other more solid flowers such as big chrysanthemums, are more striking than those with an airy, broken shape such as irises. Small details are lost from a distance and light feathery flowers make no impact.

Agapanthus, nine inches in diameter, with large aralia leaves, arranged in St Wilfrid's Parish Church, Mobberley by Molly Duerr

COLOUR

Some colours show up better than others in dimmer lighting. As a general rule, light, strong, warm colours are the best. White is the most

1. Garden flowers
arranged by Jean Taylor
in St Wilfrid's Parish
Church, Mobberley,
Cheshire

2. A pedestal arranged by Helen Caterer near the High Altar of Exeter Cathedral. By courtesy of the Dean and Chapter.

3. A simple arrange-
ment by Jean Taylor of
lilies, daisies, ivy and
hosta leaves held by a
stone angel in St
Wilfrid's Church,
Mobberley

4. Flowers on Edward
III's tomb in West-
minster Abbey. By
courtesy of NAFAS

luminous colour and shows up well especially against a dark background, but if not carefully placed white flowers appear from a distance as random blobs in a design.

Colours that contain a lot of white, such as cream, apricot, pink, show up well. Yellow is another luminous colour and it also appears to lift upwards, making it useful for churches with high roofs. Yellow-green, orange, orange-red all appear to advance towards you when seen from a distance but blues and violets normally recede, unless the blue is very bright and placed in a good light. Blue and violet are not good in the centre of an arrangement because from a distance the receding colouring looks like a hole in the middle of the design. Not all reds show up well and those with a lot of blue in them, such as violet-red rhododendrons, can look dark and heavy.

The minister may like you to use flowers of a colour that is symbolic of certain Church seasons. This is not necessary to Christian worship but may help to focus the mind on certain aspects of the church's year. However, it is not always possible to find flowers of the desired colour. It may be appropriate sometimes to use colours to suit special services, such as yellow, the symbol of youth, for a youth service, pale pink or blue for a christening.

The background of flowers should be considered. If of dark wood, lighter flowers show up the best, but against a white wall darker flowers are necessary.

LIGHTING

Some lighting shows off flowers better than others. Strip lighting is difficult, especially if it is white rather than warm-white. Reds become muddy but blue and yellow are not changed greatly. Under normal electric lighting blues are not helped but reds, oranges and yellows are satisfactory.

Dark corners need light coloured flowers and sometimes a small spotlight can be fixed permanently in position to shine gently on the flowers. This can look lovely in a dark church when the main lights are left off until the beginning of the service. The light should not be placed too close to the flowers or they will wilt.

It is better to place a flower arrangement to one side of a window as if seen against the light only the silhouette shows.

SIMPLICITY

Flowers are placed in a church to make the setting more beautiful for worship and extravagant over-decorative effects are better avoided. It is also true to say that simple beauty is more reflective and spiritual.

Some accessories can be distracting and unsuitable for the normal church service. If something is needed to balance a flower arrangement on one side of a table then it is usually more appropriate to use a bible or a candlestick. Drapes give a contrived and fussy appearance and it seems unnecessary to hide lovely stone walls or beautifully grained wood. Very decorative stained glass windows may look better if only one of the colours is picked out and used in the flowers.

> *The introduction of beautiful natural objects into our places of public worship is not done merely to satisfy the eye with pleasing forms and glowing colours ... They are introduced, or ought to be used, as appropriate incentives to kind thoughts and pure religious feelings.*
>
> F. W. BURBIDGE 1875

STYLE

Churches vary considerably in architectural style and some are a mixture of several styles. Ornate buildings need especially simple arrangements. Heavy architecture such as Norman pillars may need

Flowers from Kenya arranged by Marian Aaronson in Westminster Abbey. The anthuriums in the centre echo the shapes on the gate. By courtesy of NAFAS

'The Garden of Eden' arranged by Marian Aaronson in the Church of Upper Basildon, Pangbourne. By courtesy of Grower Books

strong massed designs and lighter architecture with more graceful arches, windows and tracery may need more delicate arrangements. Massed designs with a clear silhouette are usually the most effective in churches. In shape this may be a triangle, a circle or an oval. A massed Hogarth curve can also be effective in some positions. These shapes are peaceful to look at and give a sense of stability and dignity which is important for the atmosphere of the service. Modern churches need simple modern containers but massed arrangements of large flowers are still suitable as long as they are not fussy or insignificant. Sometimes driftwood with a bold shape arranged with a few big leaves and

Spring flowers combined with evergreens to direct attention to the Cross, arranged by Dorothy Cooke in the Parish Church of St Mary Magdalene, Knighton, Leicester

flowers is appropriate. Whatever the style it is important that the arrangement is in sympathy with the style of the church.

PLACEMENT

It is essential that flowers do not impede in any way the church service and the movements of people. The minister's movements must certainly not be hampered. It is also important that the flowers do not block the view of any member of the congregation.

The church may have certain regulations with regard to the placement of flowers and these must be obeyed. Some churches never allow flowers on the altar, others allow them except during Lent, while some permit flowers on the altar at all times. The minister may have certain preferences about the placement of flowers and it is essential to consult him about this.

Sometimes flowers can be placed so that they lead the eyes to a sacred object such as a Cross. Alternatively, they may be arranged to hide or detract from an unattractive feature in the church. Flowers may be placed in the porch but may need wiring securely if it is windy.

A bowl of flowers is a welcome sight near the entrance to the church and gives a cared-for appearance and the children enjoy flowers in their special corner. Niches are sometimes built into the walls and these are ideal especially if they can be lit. Most church flower arrangers have over the years found the best places for flowers in their own particular church.

STABILITY

The dignity of the service is important and it is most disturbing if a flower arrangement falls over. Precarious mechanics and wobbly containers should be avoided at all costs. There are some places where people may pass and brush against the flowers and unless the arrangement is stable it is likely to get knocked over. If necessary, and for peace of mind, the arrangement may be wired, or tied unobtrusively, to a permanent part of the building.

HEIGHT

Flowers are more easily seen if they are raised higher than the normal eye-level when one is standing up. This can be achieved through the use of pedestals, plinths and containers with stems. Sometimes arrangements can be placed on permanent features in the building such as high shelves, brackets or the top of a screen, when there is a ledge running across the top. High roofs tend to diminish the size and importance of flowers and so taller arrangements should be made for churches with lofty ceilings.

Flowers placed on a high wall bracket in St Wilfrid's Church, Mobberley, arranged by Merle Lowrence

Fresh flowers arranged by Mrs Donald Peachey to complement the screen in St John the Baptist Parish Church, Cirencester

Arranging the flowers

Flowers are not difficult to arrange, especially if you remember that all you are trying to do is to show the beauty of each one.

An old friend of mine, who at the age of fourteen started his working life as a gardener at Sandringham, told me that he remembers being very anxious when told that one of his duties was the arrangement of some of the flowers in the house. The head gardener at the time gave him three rules for arranging flowers and these he maintains are all you need to know:

1. Leave a little space around each flower so that its shape may be clearly seen.
2. Cut the stems different lengths so that each flower ends up at a different height in the arrangement and does not crowd another flower.
3. Turn the flowers so that they all face slightly different ways because this gives greater interest and depth to the design.

This is very good advice but I would add another point:

4. Make sure that the arrangement suits its setting in colouring, size and shape.

Arranging flowers

Scale

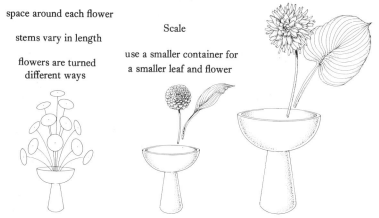

use a bigger container
for a bigger leaf and flower

space around each flower

stems vary in length

Scale

flowers are turned
different ways

use a smaller container for
a smaller leaf and flower

SELECTING FLOWERS AND LEAVES FOR AN ARRANGEMENT

It is a help to pick or buy with the flower arrangement in mind as otherwise it is easy to waste flowers.

1. *Pick or buy with restraint.* Most people tend to put too many flowers into a design, making it look cramped and over-decorative. Choose some leaves first and then buy or pick flowers to provide colour.

2. *Choose bigger flowers and leaves,* whenever available, for the larger containers. They show up better and also fewer are needed. Select leaves and flowers that are related in size, for example a large hydrangea flower is not in scale with the leaf of a rose; a big hosta or bergenia leaf would be more suitable.

3. *Consider the type of foliage.* Some flowers such as roses, gladioli and chrysanthemums have leaves on their stems and may be used without any other foliage. Often the use of just one variety of flower is very simple and effective. Other flowers, such as dahlias that have long bare stems, look better arranged with the foliage of another plant such as laurel or beech. Some flowers, for example lilac, have leaves on the stem that quickly wilt when cut and these should be removed. Instead, foliage that holds up well in water must be used for the arrangement.

COLOUR SELECTION

There are thousands of colours in the world around us and the more we become aware of colour the more of these we notice. This can make selection rather difficult but in a church arrangement there is normally a need for bright, luminous and warm colours that show up well.

An arrangement looks more interesting when it includes variations in tints, tones and shades of one colour. A tint is a colour that seems to have a lot of white in it. Tones are greyed and shades are dark and appear to have black in them. Orange for example can vary from pale apricot, which is a tint, through brilliant fiery orange to deep chocolate brown, which is orange with black in it. When flowers are seen from a distance variations between colours become less clear, and an orange and an orange-red can look very similar from the back of a church. It is better therefore to select tints and shades that are further apart, such as apricot and brown combined with a little brilliant orange.

It is also better to include several flowers in each of the colours used as this gives a greater sense of unity. A single flower of one colour looks isolated.

When several different colours are combined in one arrangement it will look more pleasing if there is a *relationship* between them. It is easy to see that apricot and orange are related, but there is also a kinship between yellow and orange. Orange contains a lot of yellow as you will see if you mix yellow and red paint together. This also means that orange is related to red but yellow and red are further apart and sometimes can be effectively linked by adding orange. All colours seem to go with nature's greens which are very amenable. When the lighting is strong enough in a church to use blue and violet you will find that they combine well. Violet paint results from mixing blue and red and so violet is akin to blue and to red. Violet, blue and pink (a tint of red) are happy together.

The container is part of the design and so the colour of the container should be linked with that of the plant material. You are safe if you choose earthy colours and black. White and brightly coloured containers are very dominant and more difficult to use with success.

White flowers are lovely in a white container, especially for a wedding, but they can be difficult to combine with other coloured flowers unless tints are chosen. These contain a lot of white and seem more related than, say, dark red and white.

You can learn so much about colour from studying nature. Sunsets, birds, flowers, butterflies and so on. have fascinating colour harmonies that may inspire the colour scheme for a flower arrangement. *The Flower Arranger's Guide to Colour Theory*, a leaflet published by NAFAS, 21a Denbigh Street, London SW1V 2HF, is an invaluable help.

The massed or bouquet style of flower arrangement is usually the most suitable for many churches. This is because it shows up better than arrangements containing a lot of space and few flowers. A round or oval outline has been used for many centuries and is not difficult to arrange; a triangle is also pleasing. The silhouette or outline is all important because this shows up clearly from a distance. Also the massed style normally suits the architecture of a church and the dignity of a service. There is no need for the outline to be rigid in appearance and soft,

A spacious arrangement in Canterbury Cathedral for the Enthronement of Archbishop Michael Ramsey

flowing designs are usually far more pleasing to look at than stiff, formal ones. When flowers are packed too closely together without room to breathe they can appear stiff. The use of long stems, especially curved ones, is a help.

Sometimes the outline of the arrangement can match the shape of surrounding arches, the tops of windows, or fan vaulting in the ceiling and this gives a sense of harmony between the church and the arrangement.

There are many beautiful shapes in plant material including those of pine cones, lilies, roses, aspidistra leaves, reeds, gourds. Every piece of plant material has an individual shape which can be generally classified into

1. elongated shapes, such as the leaves of an iris, delphinium flowers, branches of foliage or blossom, bulrushes;
2. rounded or nearly rounded shapes such as open roses, dahlias, chrysanthemums, daisies, oranges, apples;

Basic shapes

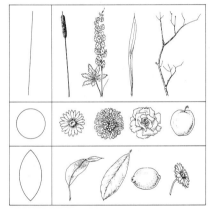

3. inbetween shapes, that are neither elongated or rounded, such as laurel leaves, half-open buds and flowers in profile. It is possible to make an arrangement using only one shape but it is usually more satisfactory to use a few of each, if they are available. Long shapes, such as branches, can be placed on the outside of the arrangement to draw your eye into the centre. Large round flowers, which are very dominant in shape, are suitable for emphasising the centre of the design. Inbetween shapes make useful stepping stones, softening the two other contrasting shapes and combining them well.

When long, spikey flowers, leaves or branches are not available a suitable bouquet style may be made from rounded flowers and oval-shaped foliage.

Making the arrangement

Make sure that the mechanics are firm before you start and if possible put the container in its final position because this makes it easier to estimate a suitable size and shape. Half fill the container with water, place nearby a box lid, or a length of polythene, for the flowers and leaves and also for rubbish. Then you are ready to begin.

You should start the arrangement wherever you like. I find it easier, when making an oval or a circular shape, to start at one side and work first upwards and then down the other side. When making a triangle I usually start with the central, tallest point. Many experienced arrangers begin by using foliage for a framework and as a setting for the flowers, which they add finally for colour. This is an economical and effective method.

OVAL AND CIRCULAR SHAPES

It may seem easier to cover the mechanics before you start by cutting short (about two inches) the stems of large plain leaves and placing them into the mechanics sideways, so that the leaves lie flat against the foam or netting. These leaves also provide a dense background for showing up the flowers. Smaller flowers, leaves and sometimes branches may be added at the sides and the top and then the largest round flowers can be placed in the centre.

A TRIANGLE

The triangle is a classical shape in Britain and very popular for churches as it seems to reach up to heaven. Place the tallest stem towards the back of the mechanics in the centre. There is no firm rule about the height but normally the flowers should look more important than the container and this can be achieved by their height. Some people use the general guide of making them about one and a half times the height of the container. This depends somewhat on the container used and the plant material. With a heavy looking container the stems should be taller than otherwise. Delicate plant material may need to be taller than heavier looking flowers. Larkspur, which is rather dainty, should be taller than stocks, when used in the same sized container. If the container seems small in relation to the selected plant material you may need to make the arrangement rather lower.

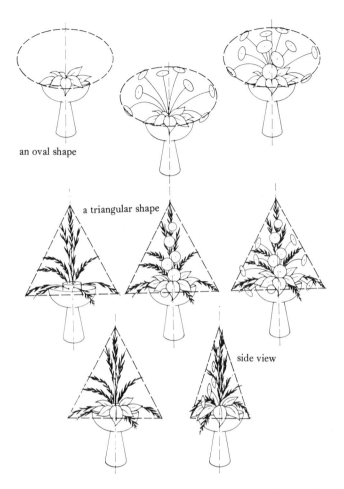

an oval shape

a triangular shape

side view

After placing 'the backbone' in position (this does not have to be stiff and straight, and a gently curved stem may be used), add two gracefully curving stems for the lower points of the triangle at each side. These need not be of the same plant material as the central stem. I then find it easier to add some large plain, flat leaves with short stems to cover the mechanics. The foliage of hosta, honesty, geranium, bergenia are all suitable. Some flowers may then be added to highlight the centre of the design and may be placed in random fashion, in a gentle curving line or in a group. The sides will now look bare and so I add stems either side. This completes a triangle from the front but perhaps the deign should be likened to a loose cone or even a pyramid, because a few stems should be placed to come forwards at the base and facing outwards at the back. This eliminates a flat back and front.

There are some useful general guidelines when making a massed shape:

1. Place the largest flowers you have in the centre facing forwards, smaller ones at the side gradually turning away from the centre and towards the back of the design. This gives a feeling of depth. Flower arrangement is like sculpture in relation to shape and it is important to work in three dimensions. Imagine the whole arrangement as a tree with the container as the trunk. From the top of the trunk, branches (or flower stems) reach out in all directions from the centre, not only upwards and sideways but forwards and backwards.
2. Place the stems so that they appear to radiate from one central point as this gives a more graceful and rhythmic appearance.
3. Allow a little space around each flower because if two are placed close together they appear to merge into each other and from a distance lose their identity.

FINISHING TOUCHES

Before leaving the arrangement go to the back and different parts of the church to look at your arrangement from various angles. It is not sensible to keep making alterations and it makes the job rather tedious. Alter major placements if really necessary and then leave it alone.

Fill the container full of water and be sure that the mechanics are covered from close quarters and from all angles. Then after tidying up any mess, sit down and enjoy the beautiful result of your efforts.

Altar flowers

Some altars are so ornate or small that flowers are superfluous. Some churches do not allow flowers on the altar. When it is the practice to use them it is normally simplicity which is the most beautiful. A few lovely flowers arranged naturally can remind us of a creation more infinite than we may understand. The altar or Communion table is the centre of worship and holds other furnishings so the minimum of flowers is appropriate. White is usually suitable, depending on the colour of the surroundings and the altar frontal. Matching pairs of arrangements may be arranged either side of the Cross. (Divide the flowers into two similar bunches first.)

It is important to cover the fair linen cloth with a sheet of polythene before beginning. Alternatively the flowers may be arranged elsewhere and then placed in position. The Cross should not be dominated by the flowers and it may be better to keep the arrangement lower in height. Equal heights in flowers and candlesticks may not be attractive.

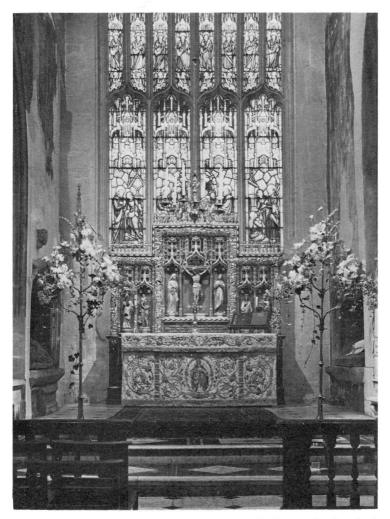

Simple flower arrangements by Sheila Macqueen leading to the altar in St John the Baptist Parish Church, Cirencester

When the Cross is placed to one side of the Communion table an arrangement may be positioned on the other. Alternatively with the cross in the middle, flowers may be arranged on one side and a bible or candlestick on the other. It is usually advisable to consult the minister about the altar flowers, unless you know the precedure, and certainly before furnishings are moved.

Lilies for an altar vase in St Wilfrid's Parish Church, Mobberley

6

Seasons and Special Occasions

The Seasons of the Year

WINTER

Winter has a poignant beauty and we are conscious of snow-covered mountains, bare branches, winter sunsets and the sparkle of frost, but there are few flowers in our gardens and although hothouse grown chrysanthemums, roses, lilies, gladioli and carnations are available all the year round they are expensive.

It is probably better to concentrate on evergreens rather than flowers, using varying textures and colours of green. Mixed evergreens can look lovely and appropriate for the season. In much earlier days greenery was used to decorate the church all the year round because few flowers were

Winter arrangements of evergreens and spring flowers by Mary Brocklehurst on the Communion Table of Barnby Gate Methodist Church, Newark. By courtesy of the Newark Advertiser

55

cultivated. Sprays of variegated ivy can cascade down from a tall container, and magnolia and camellia leaves in an urn look elegant and last well. Yew, cupressus, cedar, juniper and Western hemlock, with visually rough textures, can be combined with the smoother leaves of bergenia, and Helleborus Corsicus, the bright, yellow-splashed green of Elaeagnus 'Limelight' or the graceful leaves of Mahonia × 'Charity'. Leaves of bergenia are often shot with red and yellow in the winter and the catkins of Garrya elliptica are fascinating early in the year. A few florists flowers can sometimes be added for emphasis in the centre of an arrangement.

Brown and grey glycerined foliage and the seedheads gleaned in the summer can also be combined with a few brightly coloured flowers. Oranges, lemons, tangerines, pineapples and peppers can also provide colour. Pine cones can be wired to droop down in clusters in a design with a framework of foliage and a few stems of chysanthemums in the centre. Bare branches and driftwood can look beautiful when arranged with foliage or a few flowers.

This is a time when houseplants can be used if the church is frost free and there is sufficient light. The plants should be put as near to a window as possible except in very icy weather.

A *pot-et-fleur* makes an attractive decoration. This is a grouping of houseplants in a deep container such as a Victorian wash bowl or copper pan. Place gravel in the bowl first and sprinkle this with charcoal to keep the water sweet. Place a layer of John Innes Compost No. 2 on the gravel and then add the plants, combining several that have varying textures and colours and leaves of different shapes. Firm the plants in, using more of the compost, and fill up to within an inch of the top of the bowl. This leaves room for watering. When more colour is desirable a small deep food tin containing mechanics can be sunk into the compost to hold cut flowers. The plants should be those that enjoy the same conditions of light and moisture and plants that like very dry conditions should not be combined with those that prefer a wet soil.

Bay trees in tubs are expensive but long lasting and they may be used inside the church for decoration during winter and outside the entrance during the summer.

SPRING

After the scarcity of flowers in winter spring flowers seem especially beautiful. Spring is a time when the earth stirs once more from its winter sleep, a time of youth and new-found vigour. There are many yellow flowers and yellow green foliage. Spring flowers have a delicacy that makes them suitable for using in baskets and glass containers.

A pot-et-fleur using longlasting plants and cut flowers for winter

Stems are short and often the flowers look more attractive when combined with bare or budding branches or with driftwood. Flowers tend to be smaller than in summer and autumn and therefore need smaller containers.

Spring flowers are not as long lived as the flowers of other seasons because they prefer the cool conditions of the garden to the warmth of indoors and they may need renewing during the week. Shallow water is

A spring pedestal arranged by Doris Walne with arum lilies, eucalyptus foliage, hyacinth and willow in the Parish Church of St Mary Magdalene, Knighton, Leicester

better as deep water tends to make the stems soggy and limp. Sometimes it is a help to plant small 'gardens' in compost or moss of flowers that are still attached to their bulbs, and to include plants with roots, such as polyanthus and primulas. These gardens last longer than cut flowers.

Hyacinth, daffodil, tulip and iris bulbs may be planted in the winter in bowls and forced for bringing into the church. Amaryllis have large, striking, long-lasting flowers. From out-of-doors there are catkins of alder, willow and hazel, and the sticky buds of horse-chestnut are fascinating in texture and the manner in which they unfurl. Acer platanoides has brilliant lime green flowers that open before the leaves and there are many of these trees in the countryside. Yellow forsythia is a good colour for the church and the young leaves of Acer brilliantissimum are a wonderful peach colour in the early spring, blending beautifully with stone walls. Primroses from the garden (not from the countryside from which they are fast disappearing) can be massed in shallow bowls. Spring foliage is not long lasting and it is better to use evergreen foliage with spring flowers.

SUMMER

The scent of flowers, the fluttering of butterflies and the humming of bees, starry skies and warm still nights bring a time of garden flowers in many varieties, including lilac, poppies, peonies, and delphiniums. It is a time for finding new and unknown plants at flower shows and in people's gardens and for asking for roots of perennials when next divided.

Very tall and splendid arrangements can be made in the summer with long-stemmed delphiniums, foxgloves, eremurus, lilies, lupins, acanthus, peonies and branches of philadelphus, lime and buddleia stripped of their leaves to help them to last a long time. Plant material for pedestals is easy to find and there are big leaves such as hosta, cardoon and bergenia that last well in water. Trails of honeysuckle, periwinkle and shrub roses look lovely cascading down from a pedestal arrangement and cow parsley can be massed in country churches.

It is easy to put too many flowers into a summer design. Sometimes a mixed array, looking like a Flemish flower painting, is lovely but at other times it is restful to have arrangements of only one variety of flower. One can experiment with colour schemes such as pink with yellow, pink and blue, white and pink, yellow and white, apricot and brown or grey and so on.

At this time remember to glycerine foliage for the winter.

Dahlias, gladioli and grasses arranged for Autumn by Jane Attlee in Alvescot Church, Oxfordshire, by courtesy of the Wilts and Gloucestershire Standard

AUTUMN

This is a season of mists and sparkling cobwebs, of dew and the smell of bonfires. The mellowing beauty of plants gives a wealth of material and great inspiration. Colours have infinite variety and some of the most beautiful colour effects can be created with the many tints, tones and shades of autumn leaves.

Much of the available plant material is large in size and visually heavy in weight and the biggest containers can be brought out of the cupboard. Most plant material is long lasting and easy to condition. There is much to collect for winter, such as seedheads, grasses, cereals, gourds, bulrushes and hydrangea for drying. Coloured leaves and ferns can be pressed under the carpet. Festoons of berries may be used in arrangements and very large pedestals are easy to arrange with the wealth of large flowers, such as dahlias and chrysanthemums. Foliage arrangements can be made with leaves of many colours.

The Church's Year

It is the custom to celebrate the feasts of Christmas, Easter, Whitsuntide and Harvest by decorating the church more extensively with flowers and foliage than for normal Sundays. There are special colours that are traditionally associated with these festivals and in some churches they appear in the vestments of the clergy, the altar frontals, bible markers, the pulpit fall, the burse and the chalice veil. Smaller churches may only have one set of these but in bigger churches there may be a definite colour procedure. These colours do not necessarily have to be seen in the flowers because there is nothing symbolic about flowers as such, and it is not always possible to find the colour at the right time. Nor is the symbolism of colour necessary to divine worship but it has significance for many people and it is pleasing to follow the colours whenever possible. The flowers should anyway be in harmony with the colours used in the church during the season. It is helpful to know the colour associations but the minister should always be consulted.

ADVENT. (four Sundays before Christmas). This is the opening season of the Christian year and a time of preparation for Christ's birth at Christmas. It starts on the Sunday nearest to 30 November. Sometimes no flowers are used. Blue is the symbolic colour.

CHRISTMAS. (Christmas day and two Sundays). For the season of Christmas, starting on Christmas Day 25 December until, and including, the festival of Epiphany celebrated on 6 January and also for the following Sunday, white and gold are used.

EPIPHANY. For the remaining five Sundays of Epiphany, green is used.

SEPTUAGESIMA, SEXAGESIMA AND QUINQUAGESIMA. These are the Sundays nearest to the seventieth day, the sixtieth day and the fiftieth day before Easter, when purple or blue are used. Sometimes green is used from Septuagesima to Shrove Tuesday.

LENT. This includes six Sundays and lasts for forty days before Easter, not including Sundays. It is a time of penitence when purple or blue are used and often no flowers are placed in the church, but this is a matter of custom.

GOOD FRIDAY. As this is a day of atonement no flowers are used and black is the colour.

EASTER DAY. For Easter day and for five following Sundays gold and white are used.

WHIT SUNDAY. From Whit Sunday until Trinity Sunday red is the colour.

TRINITY SUNDAY. Gold is used.

THE SUNDAY AFTER TRINITY. For this Sunday, and twenty-two following Sundays, green is the colour. (Further details about the Christian Calendar may be found in a book of this name published by Weidenfeld and Nicolson.)

White and gold altar frontals are used for all special events such as dedication of the church, ordination, confirmation, weddings, Harvest Festival and the feast of the Saints, except those of the Martyrs, when red frontals are used. A mixture of all colours or white and red is sometimes used on All Saints' Day.

IDEAS FOR CHRISTMAS

This is a really festive time and most people love Christmas decorations. Evergreens such as holly, ivy, yew, cupressus, juniper, elaeagnus, camellia, magnolia, cedar and hemlock, with varying textures and shades of green, always seem appropriate in the church especially against cream stone walls. Garlands and topiary trees of greenery and cones of fruit may be used (see page 00). There is a yellow berried holly (Ilex aquifolium bacciflava), as well as the usual one with red berries, which looks beautiful with the gold and white altar frontal which is used at Christmas.

For a change the Christmas tree may be hung with fruit, but the use of glass ornaments on trees is a matter of custom in each church. Some of the loveliest trees I have seen use one definite colour scheme, and, to conform to the Christmas colours, a green tree with all gold ornaments looks very beautiful. Alternatively, gold and silver, red and gold, white and silver, gold and white, may be used as a change from the usual multi-coloured decorations. Green glass ornaments tend to be made of an unnatural green that does not go with evergreens, and blue and purple ornaments are rather cold in appearance. Lights are sometimes used on the tree and these may have bulbs of one colour to match the colour scheme. I remember with delight a star constructed by my father on the top of the church Christmas tree. Each point lit up in turn as we sang the verses of a Christmas carol until finally the star and all the lights were switched on in the last verse. It was like magic to us children.

Aerosol containers containing gold, silver and copper paint are used extensively at Christmas time to spray natural plant material, such as evergreens, dried flowers and leaves. It is a matter of opinion whether these are suitable for the church and the minister should be consulted. If overdone it tends to nullify the natural beauty of plant material so that it looks artificial and lifeless. A lovely effect however may be obtained by spraying very lightly so that the paint is hardly discernible and appears merely as a dusting to give a highlight. Sometimes two colours may be sprayed on, such as silver on gold. This gives an interesting effect on glycerined foliage if lightly done. Artificial snow can be attractive when sprayed with restraint but my own preference for church decorations is natural greenery, fruit and a few simple flowers such as the single white chrysanthemum 'Bonnie Jean', or white Christmas roses. White lilies look beautiful on the altar.

Candles give a lovely, mellow light for a candlelight service and a variety of holders is available so that the candle is enclosed and safe. The holders range from copies of old lamps to modern glass covers and may be surrounded with greenery, flowers and ribbons. They look really festive. Oil lamps and in seaside and country churches hurricane lamps can be used to give a welcome in each window.

Small Christmas trees also look effective when placed in each window and bay trees, decorated with bows, can be placed at the entrance to the church. Good ribbon should be used and each bow should be well made. It usually looks better if the bow is not tied but made by crossing over

An oil lamp with holly, cones and hellebores for Christmas

the two ends of a yard of ribbon until loops are formed and then wiring the centre tightly. This creates a knot effect and the same wire may be used to secure the bow wherever it is placed. Tails of ribbon may be added by twisting a wire tightly around the centre of a second yard of ribbon and placing it close to the bow.

Glitter, which looks like frost, can be bought in tubes at Christmas time. To make it adhere to plant material, such as seedheads and leaves, spray them with clear varnish or hair spray and quickly scatter on the glitter. It is better to do this over newspaper in order to catch the excess glitter.

It is important that the church at Christmas is decorated with taste and dignity and does not look tawdry, over-decorated or like a Christmas party. Fresh plant material is always in good taste. The crib scene is beloved by children and should be set at a level where they can easily see it. It may be displayed on a matting base with a few simple flowers or some natural greenery placed nearby, and set out by the children.

EASTER

Yellow is associated with Easter and it is a time when daffodils and narcissus are plentiful. Hazel, alder and willow catkins can be added for height. Primula and polyanthus can be placed low down in massed groups. Laurel and elaeagnus look lovely with yellow flowers. Arum lilies are traditionally placed on many altars. The leaves are not normally sold with the flowers because they are needed to feed the bulb for providing next year's flowers. Additional foliage from laurel, fatsia japonica or aspidistra may be used with the arums to soften the look of the bare stems.

WHITSUNTIDE

This is a time when the church is not decorated as extensively as at Christmas and Easter. Red gladioli look dramatic arranged alone, massed and pointing to Heaven, to represent the coming of the Holy Spirit in tongues of flame.

Early summer blossom is available and branches laden with blossom look lovely arranged without other plant material. The flowers can be encouraged to open earlier than normal if branches with mature buds are brought into the house beforehand.

HARVEST FESTIVAL

This is a feast of thanksgiving for the bounty of the earth, and a time of great plenty in the land. Decoration of the church is easy because of the abundance of fruit, flowers and leaves, but for this reason it can all too

An expressive Easter arrangement of driftwood, thorns, lilies, freesias and iris by Mary Williams

Gladioli arranged by Margery Chapman

easily look like a Saturday market scene. A feeling of plenteousness is certainly appropriate but it should be controlled and have a sense of design. This is best achieved by concentrating the gifts of fruit and vegetables into specific containers such as barrows, tubs, handcarts, and baskets, filled to overflowing. They should be placed in a position where the movements of the clergy and congregation are not impeded. The flowers look better when concentrated into a few large arrangements with restful spaces in between them, rather than many small designs.

There are dahlias, gladioli, roses, chrysanthemums, Michaelmas daisies, fruit of all kinds, branches of berried shrubs and autumn-coloured leaves in great variety and many people bring gifts. Some ministers prefer tins of food to be given instead of perishable fruits and vegetables and these may be displayed on hessian covered tables. Cereals may be symbolically included in the decorations of the church. If you want a sheaf of corn it is essential to contact a farmer ahead of time as the combine harvester does not produce the old-fashioned sheaves we like for the church. Farmers will often provide a small sack of seed corn and a bag of roots such as swedes and mangolds to place in the porch.

Fruit and vegetables such as red and green apples, grapes, melons, crab-apples, marrows, onions, pears and carrots look lovely but are not easy to arrange. They look better when each variety is grouped so that in a design the round forms are in the centre, the oval forms outside these and the more elongated and smaller shapes, such as carrots or grapes, are placed at the extremities. A few leaves placed amid the fruit softens the rather solid appearance.

Gourds are very decorative, though inedible, and these may be grown easily. There is also beautiful wild plant material but it is important to pick only plentiful flowers and fruits. There are many sprays of blackberries, hips and old-man's-beard. All the colours of orange, red, scarlet, purple, yellow, brown and green make a resplendent and joyful setting and Harvest Festival is a happy occasion.

> . . . when ye have gathered in the produce of the land, ye shall keep the feast of the Lord seven days . . . and ye shall take on the first day the fruit of goodly trees, branches of palm trees and boughs of leafy trees and willows of the brook.

LEVITICUS 23:39,40

Family Occasions

WEDDINGS

The guests at a wedding have a long while to look at the flowers in the church while they await the arrival of the bride. The flowers make a beautiful setting for the wedding service. Some brides are happy to have the flowers that are already in the church, but others like extra flowers. It is important that the bride is consulted as it is her special day and she may have a preference for flowers and colours. However it is almost certain that she will need the guidance of the person who arranges the flowers.

The number of arrangements depends on the amount of money that

Wedding flowers arranged by Alex Church in Canterbury Cathedral

the family wish to spend and an estimate should be given. Flowers on or near the altar are desirable and there can also be a number of pedestals according to the cost, which depends upon the season. It is a good idea to quote a price for one pedestal based on the number and type of flowers, the mechanics and any special effects such as bows. The flower arranger may add a fee. It is usually better if the arranger is experienced so that the cost of flowers, the positioning of arrangements and other details are easily worked out.

69

The position of the arrangements depends on the church but the view of the congregation should not be obscured. Pedestals can be placed near the altar, but any used further down the church should be positioned carefully. A small arrangement near the entrance acts as a welcome and when the bridal party return down the aisle it is pleasant to have an arrangement at the end of the church. Sometimes for a big wedding the bride likes posies at the pew ends. Flowers placed on every window sill tend to give an over-decorative appearance and it is better to concentrate the flowers into one or more large arrangements. A small posy on the table where the register is signed looks charming.

HEIGHT. It is important to place the flowers so that they can be seen above the heads of standing guests. Pedestals and shelves may be used and the top of a screen, if it has a ledge, is a good place for a cascade of flowers arranged in hidden bread tins. Swags of fresh plant material may be hung on the walls and tall topiary trees (see page 00) may give an elegant appearance.

COLOUR. Usually the family like the flowers to match the colours of the bridal party, but flowers are not always available in the desired colours. It is better to decide on the colour of the flowers before that of the bridesmaids' dresses. Fabric in many colourings is always available and easier to obtain than seasonal flowers.

White flowers are suitable and a touch of the colour of the bridesmaids' dresses can be added in the centre of the arrangement. Red, using all the available shades mixed together, is lovely in the winter. Blues can be difficult to obtain unless it is delphinium or hydrangea time. To make a completely harmonious picture the colours of the church including the walls, carpet, altar and curtains should be considered so that the guests see an overall pleasing colour scheme.

After the wedding it is normal for the flowers to be left in the church for the Sunday services but this is for the bride's family and the minister to decide.

The following is a short list of flowers that are available in various colours from time to time, but a florist or gardener should be contacted about availability. Some plants are obtainable both from florists and gardens.

White and cream

Florist's flowers	*Garden flowers*	
carnation	Solomon's seal	prunus
rose	marguerite	hydrangea
delphinium	campanula	snowberry

lily
chrysanthemum
gladiolus
narcissus
larkspur
orchid
iris
tulip
gerbera
peony
gypsophila
double freesia

lilac
azaleas
magnolia
mock orange
rhododendron
phlox
spiraea
camellia
dahlia
honeysuckle

viburnum
hellebore
cow parsley
old-man's-beard
snowball tree
laurustinus
hosta
tobacco plant
broom
hyacinth

Blue

Florist's flowers
delphinium
scabious
cornflower
iris

Garden flowers
agapanthus
campanula
lupin
sea holly
hydrangea
globe thistle
phlox
hyacinth

Mauve

Florist's flowers
larkspur
gladiolus
carnation
freesia
stock
tulip
orchid

Garden flowers
lilac
dahlia
foxglove
delphinium
phlox
allium
lupin

cobaea scandens
Michaelmas daisy
rose

Pink

Florist's flowers
carnation
orchid
stock
gladiolus
anthurium
rose
peony
larkspur
alstroemaria
lily

Garden flowers
camellia
dahlia
hydrangea
weigela
spiraea
rhododendron
escallonia
phlox
prunus
poppy

snapdragon	hostas
nerine	hyacinth
amaryllis	
pyrethrum	
protea	
freesia	
tulip	

Orange and peach

Florist's flowers	*Garden flowers*	
strelitzia	rhododendron	Chinese lantern
gerbera	marigold	autumn leaves
clivia	zinnia	red hot poker
rose	iris	berries
chrysanthemum	foxglove	
gladioli	azalea	
stock	eremurus	
carnation	dahlia	
tulip	montbretia	
alstroemaria	crown imperial	

Yellow

Florist's flowers	*Garden flowers*
gladioli	achillea
carnation	forsythia
rose	trollius
chrysanthemum	broom
tulip	daffodil
lily	doronicum
gerbera	winter jasmine
mimosa	rhododendron
iris	red hot poker
freesia	fennel
alstroemaria	hyacinth

Red

Florist's flowers	*Garden flowers*	
gladiolus	geranium	rhododendron
rose	snapdragon	berries
carnation	autumn leaves	
poinsettia	lobelia cardinalis	
amaryllis	dahlia	
anthurium	peonie	
tulip	zinnia	
gerbera	sweet William	

Green

Garden flowers	*Grey foliage*
zinnia	cedar
bells-of-Ireland	onopordum
euphorbia	artichokes
gladiolus	senecio greyii
alchemilla mollis	rosa rubrifolia
cobaea scandens	cineraria maritima
hellebore	hosta sieboldiana
angelica	
artichoke	
love-lies-bleeding	
tobacco plant	
tulip	
orchid (florist)	
lime	
Norway maple	

FUNERALS

Flowers can be a tiny comfort at times of great sorrow. They say what people find difficult to express in words – that God is forever giving new life, and that we are part of the world of nature with its continuous cycle of life and death. Those who are going through a time of great stress can look at flowers in the church, and momentarily take their minds away from their deep sorrow. A very simple arrangement of flowers such as roses or lilies is suitable. It could be appropriate to use flowers from the garden of the person who has died.

CHRISTENINGS

Dainty flowers look delightful at a christening and should be provided by arrangement with the parents. If they are placed on the font it is important that room is left for the minister to put his hands in the water used for the baptism. The flowers should not crowd the top of the font and are better put at one side. Tiny flowers in pastel colours, such as pale pink, blue, white, yellow and cream, are the most charming for the occasion. They could be Carol roses, white daisies, lilies of the valley, forget-me-nots, primroses, honeysuckle, gypsophila.

7

Growing Plant Material for the Church

It is symbolic that the story of the Bible begins and ends in a garden,

ROSETTE CLARKSON

Many members of the congregation may be happy to grow plant material for the church flower arrangements, especially if they know what is wanted. This can be a big economy, spreads the work and arouses much interest. Some plants are more useful than others because they may last well when cut; provide berries or seedheads; preserve or dry successfully; provide reliable foliage. In a church the roof is higher than at home, spaces are larger, light can be dimmer. This means that taller stems, definite shapes, brighter colours are more effective. If a number of people set aside a small part of their garden to grow flowers for the church one member's garden is not denuded of colour to provide cut flowers.

It is disappointing both for the grower and the flower arranger if unsuitable flowers arrive for the arrangements. This can be avoided with a little communication and an article in the parish magazine, a duplicated letter, or a small booklet made available as a handout, could list the varieties of flowers and leaves that are of use at different times of the year. There could be added a few hints on 'how and when to cut flowers' to make things easier for the flower arranger, such as:

the advantage of cutting in the evening;
the need for long stems;
how to cut stems on the slant;
the necessity to place the flower stems in deep, tepid water at once;
cutting buds that show colour and not mature, open flowers;
how to pack plant material;

Hardy perennials

These provide a great variety of cut flowers, chiefly in the summer. Many perennials also have useful foliage and seedheads and some may be dried or preserved with glycerine. Many churchgoers have suitable perennials in the garden. Every two or three years when the plants need to be divided, owners may be able to give clumps to other people to grow. An offer to collect and distribute these is useful, or a day may be arranged in the autumn or spring for a big plant exchange.

Suitable hardy perennials for church use include:

Achillea 'Coronation Gold', deep yellow, dries well;

Alchemilla mollis (Lady's mantle), long flowering, small yellow flowers;

Angelica archangelica, short-lived, seeds itself, tall green seedheads;

Arum italicum (a form of Lords and Ladies), good winter leaves;

Astilbe, plume-like heads in several colours;

Bergenia (Elephant's ear), large, short-stemmed leaves for all the year;

Chrysanthemum maximum (Shasta daisy) 'Wirral Supreme' a double white;

Cortaderia (Pampas grass), tall, everlasting grass;

Crambe cordifolia, very big;

Curtonus paniculatus, a cormous plant with giant montbretia-type flowers;

Cynara cardunculus (Cardoon), grey-green leaves, for pedestals. C. scolymus (Globe artichoke) for seedheads.

Delphinium elatum

Doronicum (Leopard's bane) 'Harpur Crew', yellow, daisy-type flowers;

Eremurus (Foxtail lily) tall, spikey flowers;

Eryngium (Sea-holly) dries well, E. alpinum, fluffy bracts; E. giganteum (Miss Willmott's ghost) big (dies after flowering);

Euphorbia (Spurge), E. polychroma bright yellow in spring, E. robbiae rosette-shaped foliage, E. characias, E. wulfenii;

Filipendula, closely related to spiraea and useful 'filler;

Helenium autumnale and Helianthus decapetalus, long-lasting, daisy-type flowers;

Helleborus foetidus, apple green flowers in winter;

Hosta (Plantain lily), summer foliage in many variations;

Iris, the bearded or flag iris have useful leaves and flowers;

Kniphofia (Red-hot poker), white, yellow and red flowers;

Lobelia cardinalis, long stemmed with brilliant red flowers;

Lychnis chalcedonica (Maltese cross), useful scarlet heads;

Macleaya cordata (Plume poppy), tall stems, tiny white flowers;

Miscanthus sinensis variegatus (Giant grass);

Paeonia (Peony);

Papaver orientale (Oriental poppy);

Phlox paniculata, filler, many colours;

Phormium tenax (New Zealand flax), tall foliage for all year;

Physalis franchetii (Chinese lantern), autumn seedpods;
Phytolacca (Poke-weed), blackberry-like fruits (poisonous);
Polygonatum x hybridum (Solomon's seal), arched stems, late spring;
Polystichum setiferum 'Divisilobum', hardy fern;
Pyrethrum, daisy-like, long-lasting;
Scabiosa (Scabious), yellow, blue and white flowers;
Sedum (Stonecrop) 'Autumn Joy', long season, green then red flower;
Senecio maritima 'Diamond', light grey leaves;
Solidago (Golden rod);
Trollius (Globe flower), buttercup-like flowers;
Verbascum, tall stems;
Vinca major (Greater periwinkle) trails.

Annuals, biennials

The children in the church congregation may enjoy growing annuals
because they grow quickly and are gay and pretty. They might enjoy
participating in a 'Grow for the Church' campaign. Local nurserymen
also may be willing to grow specified annuals for the church. Many annuals, though lovely, are not longlasting for use in church arrangements,
unless they are renewed during the week, but the following can be very
useful.

HA . . . hardy annual, HHA . . . half-hardy annual, B . . . biennial

Antirrhinum, HHA, a useful tall flower, double Madam Butterfly has
many colours but choose tall varieties;
Amaranthus caudatus (Love-lies-bleeding), HHA, dark red and green
varieties which make graceful trailers to drop down the sides of
containers. Also dries well;
Callistephus (China aster), HHA, mixed packets;
Calendula (English marigold), HA, yellow, white, orange;
Chrysanthemum carinatum (annual chrysanthemum), HA;
Coreopsis tinctoria, HA, yellow flowers;
Cucurbita pepo (ornamental gourd), HHA, useful for harvest
festivals;
Delphinium consolida (Larkspur), HA, D. ajacis (Rocket larkspur),
HA;
Dianthus barbatus (Sweet William), B;
Digitalis (Foxglove), B;
Dipsacus fullonum (Teasel), B;
Gaillardia, HA, red and yellow daisy flower;
Helianthus annuus (Sunflower), HA, H. debilis, HA;

Humulus japonicus variegata (variegated hop), HA, good trailer;
Lathyrus oderatus (Sweet pea), HA;
Lunaria annua (Honesty), B, good leaves for winter and seedheads;
Lupinus (Lupin), HA;
Matthiola (annual stock), HHA;
Moluccella laevis (Bells of Ireland), HHA, green, glycerines well;
Nicotiana affinis (Tobacco plant), HHA;
Onopordum acanthium (Scotch thistle), B, O. arabicum, B;
Papaver somniferum (Opium poppy), HA;
Rudbeckia (Cone flower), HHA;
Salvia horminum, HA;
Scabiosa atropurpurea (Sweet scabious), HA, many colours;
Tithonia (Mexican sunflower), HHA, very bright orange;
Tagetes erecta (African marigold), HHA, yellow and orange;
Verbascum bombyciferum, B, grey leaves;
Zinnia elegans, HHA;

Roses

So many people grow roses that it is unnecessary to ask members of the congregation to grow them specially for the church. The old roses are very lovely for arrangements but do not last. Modern roses are lasting if they are picked in bud and conditioned well, but, it is unlikely that they will last a full week. Some of the better ones for lasting are:

Amberlight, floribunda, deep orange, small;
Constance Spry, modern shrub, pink, large, old shape;
Ernest H. Morse, Hybrid Tea, rich turkey red;
Fragrant Cloud, Hybrid Tea, geraniumlake;
Grandpa Dickson, HT, yellow;
Mischief, HT, coral-salmon;
Pascali, HT, white;
Peace, HT, light yellow;
Queen Elizabeth, floribunda, clear pink;
Rosa rubrifolia, species, grey leaves;
Rosa moyesii, 'Geranium' species, good hips;
Super Star, HT, vermilion;
Sutters Gold, HT, orange shaded red;
Virgo, HT, white;
Wendy Cussons, HT, cerise;
Whisky Mac, HT, gold;

Tubers, bulbs, corms

DAHLIAS

Dahlias last well if they are picked when young and they are invaluable for harvest festival decorations. Most people grow a few in the garden and it is easy to find varieties which suit the church in colour and size. The larger cactus and decorative groups may be the most useful, but some ball and pompom dahlias can make attractive smaller arrangements.

LILIES

Lilies always seem so perfectly suited to church decoration. They last well, are a good size and have lovely shapes. They are easy to grow and many are hardy. Lilium candidum, the Madonna lily, has been cultivated for 3,500 years and is often seen in Renaissance paintings as it was the symbol of the Madonna. Arums are traditionally used in the church at Easter and may be grown specially. Their dignity and simplicity suit churches.

There are many lovely lilies for cutting and a visit to your local nurseryman when the lily buds arrive will show you from illustrations what you are buying

These are useful:

Lilium auratum, the golden-rayed lily of Japan, stem-rooting, white with brown spots;

L. candidum, the Madonna lily, base-rooting, lime tolerant, white;

L. Bright Star, stem-rooting, lime tolerant, white with apricot centre;

L. henryi, stem-rooting, likes lime, plant 8 inches deep, deep orange-yellow;

L. Limelight, stem-rooting, flowers last well, yellow;

L. longiflorum, stem-rooting, lovely shape, white;

L. pardalinum, very hardy, base-rooting, easily grown, orange Turk's cap flowers;

L. regale, stem-rooting, lime tolerant, white with yellow shading, purple outside;

Aurelian, Mid-Century, Fiesta and Olympic hybrids, the speciosum and tigrinum varieties;

Zantedeschia (Arum lily), out-of-doors in mild districts.

SPRING BULBS

So many spring bulbs are already grown in gardens that special planting for the church is unnecessary. However, it is most useful in the rather

Yellow lilies with hosta leaves in St Wilfrids Parish Church, Mobberley

79

bleak time after Christmas when flowers are scarce and expensive, and before outdoor bulbs flower, to have some early forced bulbs. Hyacinth bulbs planted in the first week of September could be ready for this time when a change from evergreens is welcome. Narcissus, irises and small bulbous flowers are not really bold enough for the church but the early double tulips, hyacinth and daffodils grow well indoors and are a refreshing breath of spring during the cold weather.

Members of the congregation may already plant bulbs indoors and should be willing to include an extra bowl or two for the church. Alternatively bulbs for forcing may be bought from the flower fund and shared between several members.

The bulbs can be planted in suitable bowls for display or in plastic buckets or clay pots. These may be dropped into decorative outer containers from the church flower arrangement cupboard or the bulbs may be completely removed and replanted in the church containers. Fresh, green moss looks attractive placed over the soil. It is more practical to leave the flowers attached to the bulbs and not to cut them off because they last longer left this way. Also the leaves and stems can die down naturally, nourishing the bulb for another year.

When the flower is over the bulbs may be planted in the churchyard to finally die down. Next year they will provide cut flowers later in the season because they cannot be forced again and new bulbs must be bought for this purpose each year.

If members wish to plant outdoor tulips for the church the longer stemmed varieties are more suitable including:

Parrot tulips, with fantastic feathery flowers in April and May;
Rembrandt tulips, flowering in May with exotic striped colours and long stems;
Tulipa viridiflora, flowering in April and early May with lovely colours laced with green;
Darwin tulips and Darwin hybrids, flowering in May with some of the largest flowers and longest stems;
Lily flowering tulips in April with long stems;
Double early tulips (like peonies) in April.

ALLIUMS

These ornamental relations of the onion have exciting flowers from May to July which turn into spectacular seedheads, and their cylindrical form is especially clear and definite. They have long lives in the garden and need not be lifted.

Allium aflatuense, pale mauve, 3–4 inch umbels, May and June;
A. albopilosum, lilac pink, 6 inch umbels, June;

A. giganteum, deep lilac 4 inch umbels, June;

A. siculum, bell shaped, white flowers clustered, May–June;

A. rosenbachianum, dense purple 5 inch umbels in May –June.

HIPPEASTRUM (AMARYLLIS)

The Barbados lily has been described as the 'Queen' of bulbs. One or more, 5- to 6-inch wide flowers appears at the top of long straight stems. They are certainly beautiful, pink, orange, flame red, white and sometimes striped in colour. Bulbs up to 6 inches in diameter are expensive to buy but they have many years of growth if treated correctly. They are spectacular in a church and could be cut for an arrangement or placed, with the bulb in a pot, in a decorative outer container. The bulbs are not hardy and must be grown indoors. When used as a cut flower leave half the stem on the bulb.

GLADIOLUS

Gladioli are excellent cut flowers and a good size for church arrangements. There are many plain colours and some with more than one colour in a large range. They should be cut when the first floret is just opening for long life as a cut flower. Four leaves at least should be left intact after cutting the flower spike to maintain the development of the new corm. They often look their best arranged without other flowers in great fan shapes.

Shrubs

The foliage of shrubs is invaluable for use in winter when no perennial foliage is available. Many shrubs also have lovely flowers and berries that can be used in church arrangements. Shrubs are of course a long term investment and so if possible should be planted in the churchyard to last for generations. As they are slow growing the people who plant them may not reap the benefit for some years but they are a good investment for future church flower arrangers. Evergreens are an especially good choice as they look green and attractive in the churchyard all the year.

It is a mistake to think that shrubs should never be cut for decoration. Indiscriminate hacking is a disaster but careful cutting encourages new growth in the same way as pruning. Cutting should be the responsibility of one or two people only, then the shrubs should thrive without any problem.

In view of the permanency and expense of shrubs, careful choice is important, not only for their use in decoration but for their appearance in the churchyard. Advice from a local nurseryman is a help and shrubs should be selected with the climate in mind. This may be windy, exposed or cold. Consider also the type of soil because some shrubs do not like a lot of lime. A testing kit for testing acidity and alkalinity is available from garden centres. When cutting for flower arrangements there are certain guidelines which will protect the shrub.

Cut off a branch where there is another growing close by as this will grow on with more space and light.

Cut immediately above a new shoot which will replace the branch removed.

Think of the shape of the branch for a flower arrangement so that unsuitable branches are not cut and then wasted.

Cut less than may be needed and then return for more if necessary.

Some useful shrubs to grow. E: Evergreen D: Deciduous

Acerpseudoplatanus 'Brilliantissimum', D, apricot-coloured spring foliage;

Acer platanoides (Norway maple), D, tree with brilliant green flowers in April, before the leaves;

Aucuba japonica (Spotted laurel), E;

Buddleia davidii (Butterfly bush), D, flowers July to October;

Buxus (Box), E, small lasting foliage for making topiary trees and cones;

Choisya ternata (Mexican orange), E, a south wall in the north, rosettes of foliage;

Cotoneaster 'Cornubia', semi E, clusters of scarlet berries in autumn; C. franchetii, berries along the stem, not usually eaten by the birds;

Cytisus (Broom), D, C. albus long arching sprays;

Elaeagnus E, E. pungens 'Maculata' green leaves splashed with gold. 'Variegata' green leafed with cream edges, faster growing is variegated E. x ebbingei 'Limelight';

Escallonia, E, branches of flowers in July;

Fatsia japonica, E, large leaves for pedestals;

Fatshedera lizei, E, can be used as ground cover if pegged down, plain leaves;

Griselinia littoralis, E, shelter in cold gardens, good near the sea, light green foliage;

Hedera (Ivy), E, most churchyards contain ivy, if not, start some for trails;

Hydrangea, D, late summer flowers which dry, in lovely colours, and a useful size;

Ilex (Holly), E, I. aquifolium 'Golden King', gold-margined leaves and I.a 'Silver Queen', silver-edged leaves; I.a. 'Bacciflava' yellow berries (if a male holly is planted nearby such as Silver Queen);

Laurus nobilis (Bay) E;

Ligustrum ovaliforium 'Aureo-marginatum' (Golden privet), E, useful variegated foliage all year;

Lonicera japonica (Japanese Honeysuckle), E, climber for trails;

Mahonia x 'Charity', E, graceful leaves;

Skimmia japonica, E, bright green foliage and red berries if a male and female are planted together;

Sorbus aria (Whitebeam), D, young silver leaves in spring;

Symphoricarpus rivularis 'Constance Spry' (Snowberry), white winter berries;

Viburnum tinus (Laurustinus), E;

Weigela florida 'Variegata', D, flowers in May, long branches;

The use of wild plant material

Wild flowers are lovely, especially in a country church. However, many wild flowers are likely to be extinct very soon, unless great care is taken to conserve them. The habit of *not* picking the flora of the countryside should be encouraged. This is a complete change of thought for older people who in their childhood may have made collections of wild material for village flower shows and regarded this as fair and economical 'gleaning'. People are asked by conservationists not to pick certain varieties and lists may be obtained from local conservation societies. This is a wise move that should be supported with vigour by everyone who cares about our beautiful, natural world.

> *I speak on behalf of the next generation*
> *Leave them a flower, some grass and a hedgerow*
> *A hill and a dale, a view to the sea*
> *These things are not ours to destroy,*
> *A gift given once for eternity*

A FOLK-SINGER

There are a few plants which grow in abundance and things such as pine cones, that could be used in church in small quantities and only where they are plentiful. Permission should be obtained from the owner of the land where applicable.

beech sprays for preserving, from large trees, ivy trails;
berries from the hedge-rows;
bracken with autumn colouring;

bulrushes, pine cones;
catkins of alder, hazel and pussy willow;
Queen Anne's lace, grasses;
driftwood from lake-side, seaside, woodland;
foxgloves, both flowers and seedheads;
sycamore leaves, red when young, they last if put in water at once.

Houseplants

I am surprised that houseplants are not placed in churches more often.
They are economical because they last. They are unsuitable for dark
churches but grow well in reasonable light. If frost-free there are many
that live without heat. A house plant specialist can advise on suitable
plants for different situations and a knowledgeable person should give
consistent care. The following are easy:

ivies	rhoicissus	tradescantia
aspidistra	monstera deliciosa	cholorophytum
cissus antarctica	ficus robusta	sansevieria
fatshedera		
philodendron bippinnatifidum		
peperomia		

8

Preserved and Dried Plant Material

I wonder if we would prize flowers so much if they lived indefinitely. Perhaps it is the transient life of a flower that makes it so precious. We wonder over and over again at their brief and delicate beauty. There are successful methods of preserving flowers and leaves so that they keep their shape and some of their colour but, whatever the method, the living quality cannot be prolonged.

How appropriate are dried flowers in church? My own feeling is that

Fresh yellow chrysanthemums arranged with preserved leaves, dried artichoke heads and gold achillea in a copper urn

the living quality of fresh flowers reminds of the astonishing loveliness of the natural world created by God. We see 'heaven in a wild flower', and this to me is the most important reason for placing fresh flowers in our churches. Can we have quite the same feeling of wonder about plant material that has been treated to last beyond its normal life span?

This does not mean that dried and preserved leaves and flowers have no use in church flower arrangements. On the contrary, when winter comes they are invaluable. Preserved foliage can be combined with fresh flowers, or a few dried seedheads can be arranged with fresh leaves. In other words they are excellent in a supporting role rather than featured alone.

The terms used by flower arrangers for plant material that has been treated to last are *preserved* and *dried*.

Preserving plant material

Preservation refers to replacing the water, normally present in the tissues of plant material, with glycerine. This prevents the leaf or flower from shrivelling, it remains supple and pliable and keeps its shape. Unfortunately few flowers can be preserved but many leaves can be treated and the results last for years and can be used over and over again. The great advantage is that preserved plant material comes to little harm when placed in water or foam, so that it can be used with fresh flowers.

The colour of the leaves changes as the water evaporates from the tissues and is replaced with glycerine. Most leaves turn a shade of brown varying from cream to almost black according to the type of plant material. A few leaves may turn dark green or purple-grey. Fortunately brown looks lovely with brightly coloured flowers. Beech, for example, can vary in colour from mahogany brown to light gold and looks attractive when arranged with a few orange, single chrysanthemums or brilliant scarlet dahlias.

METHODS OF PRESERVING

The recipe is simple

>1 part glycerine,
>2 parts hot water,
>Mix together well,
>Place the ends of branches in the mixture.

A bottle of glycerine can be bought from any chemist. Pour it into a wide-necked preserving jar and then fill the bottle twice over with hot water. Plants cannot take up undiluted glycerine as it is too thick which is why water should be added. Glycerine will mix with cold water but

Preserving with glycerine

pour glycerine into a jar

add twice as much hot water

stir well

remove crowded, damaged and lower leaves

place in glycerine

single leaves in glycerine solution

mop heavy leaves with the solution

hang up strong stemmed flower to dry

takes longer and more stirring is necessary. Stirring is essential as otherwise the heavier glycerine sinks to the bottom of the jar and the stem ends do not take it up.

The glycerine mixture can be used in two ways: branches can be stood in it so that it is taken up by the stem and gradually reaches the leaves; single leaves may be submerged in the solution so that it goes straight into the leaf's tissues.

1. *Method for branches*

Choose branches of any length with good shape.

Trim away damaged leaves so that glycerine is not wasted. Cut off lower branches so that the main branch can stand easily in the jar.

Scrape 2 inches of outer bark from woody stems and slit up all hard stems for about an inch, using flower scissors.

Stand the end of the branch in the warm glycerine which should reach at least one inch up the stem end. Top up if the jar runs dry.

Place the jar in a cool, dry place.

Very thick leaves like aspidistra should be mopped with the solution on the outside before standing them in it. This prevents them from drying out at the tips.

2. *Method for single leaves*

Select a perfect leaf and wash it if necessary.

Pour the glycerine mixture into a shallow bowl and push the leaf under it.

If it floats place a pebble or two on top.

WHEN TO PRESERVE

Neither very young nor old foliage take up glycerine successfully, and the majority of leaves should be treated in June, July and August when they are mature. It is too late to preserve with glycerine once leaves are showing autumn colour because the plant is then preparing for winter and is not carrying moisture of any kind to its leaves. Evergreens are often better treated in winter, if you can find perfect specimens, otherwise choose older leaves during the summer months. It is interesting to experiment with various types of foliage and the glycerine is not wasted if it is not taken up.

WHEN IS A LEAF FULLY TREATED?

People worry about when to take the foliage out of the glycerine, but leaves come to little harm if left beyond the required time, which varies from a few days to several weeks according to the variety of plant, its age and the season. You can normally tell when a branch is fully treated because of the colour change. It can then be removed and the sticky ends dried with tissue. Single leaves that have been submerged should be left to drain on sheets of newspaper for a few days and then mopped with tissue.

The glycerine can be used more than once although it may darken in colour. Branches take it up more quickly if it is warmed. A quarter teaspoon of Hibitane or any mild disinfectant added to a pint of the mixture helps to prevent mould that sometimes occurs.

STORAGE

It is important to store preserved foliage in a dry place, otherwise it becomes mildewed and must be thrown away. Polythene bags are not a good idea as condensation can cause mildew . Cardboard boxes are satisfactory or the leaves can be hung up in a dry place.

If small drops of glycerine appear on the surface of a leaf (this sometimes happens with beech) it means that the foliage has been left too long in the solution. Small droplets can be wiped off with a tissue. They do little harm and the drops will disappear if the leaves are swished about in a sink of water containing a small squeeze of detergent. This is also good treatment for dusty leaves but dry them before storing.

LIGHTER COLOUR

After preservation, leaves may be placed in strong light or sunshine for a week or so. This lightens the colour of some foliage so that a range of colour variation is possible.

USE OF PRESERVED FOLIAGE

The treated foliage may be used with fresh or dried flowers in water or foam. When removed from water it should be dried well, before being stored. Single leaves may be provided with a wire for a false stem (see 0). Preserved foliage sells well at bazaars and a group of church flower arrangers could organise this.

Dried plant material

This term refers to plant material that has had the water extracted without replacing it with anything else. Many flowers and leaves shrivel as they dry out, but there is a useful group of flowers and seedheads that retain their shape because they have rigid tissue that does not collapse when dried carefully. Few leaves dry successfully and they are better preserved. Plants change colour as they dry but there are a few that retain their colour reasonably well.

Many flowers and seedheads dry on the plant naturally if left in the

A dried arrangement by Mrs F. D. M. Flowerdew blending with the wooden pulpit in All Saints Cathedral, Nairobi, Kenya, by courtesy of East Africa Standard

garden. In fact, if a herbaceous border is not cut down in the autumn, some stems stand upright all winter. The weather damages them however and for better results it is better to dry the stems indoors.

Pick perfect specimens on a dry day when *almost* mature. Remove the leaves, which normally shrivel, and bunch the stems so that the flower heads are separated to avoid them being crushed. Place an elastic band around the end of the stems. This is better than string as it tightens as the stems dehydrate and shrink. Hang the bunches in a dry place, upside down, so that the stems remain straight. The airing cupboard gives quick results but is not necessary as most plant material dries in a few days in an airy room. Some stems dry successfully when stood up in a jar. A wooden clothes airer is useful for drying a number of bunches and it can be moved about easily.

A dry place is essential for storing because sometimes the flowers re-absorb moisture. Less damage is caused from crushing if the dried stems are placed upright in a jar. If they do become crumpled, hold the flowers over the steam of a boiling kettle for a few seconds and then reshape quickly with the fingers. Stuff tissue paper into flowers with cavities.

USE IN ARRANGEMENTS

Normally dried plant material should be used in dry mechanics so that water is not reabsorbed. Really tough dried plant material can be used with fresh flowers in water but the stem may soften. To prevent this wrap the end in florist's tape or dip it in candlewax or nail polish so that the stem is sealed.

Many dried plants are too small for effective use in a church and only the larger flowers and seedheads really show up well. A selection is given below. Plant material dried by pressing under a weight or in a press is not very successful as it is too brittle and delicate for leaving in a church flower arrangement. The same applies to flowers dried in a desiccant, which is a drying agent such as alum, borax or silica gel.

Glycerine Treatment

METHOD 1 (treat only leaves unless otherwise instructed, times in weeks are approximate)

Aspidistra   12, mop, beige;

Beech   1, use green or copper, various shades;

Bells-of-Ireland   2, after flowering, remove weak tips, beige;

Box   3, beige, useful for cones;

Choisya ternata   3, beige;

Escallonia   2, long sprays can be treated;

Eucalyptus   2, purple-grey;

Foxglove   2, seedheads, tall stems can be treated;

Hellebore   2, the Corsican variety is best;

Hydrangea   2, flowers, when mature not dry, with woody stems;

Iris   2, seedpods;

Laurel   3, dark brown;

Lime   2, flowers, remove leaves;

Oak   2, beige;

Old-man's-beard   2, just before flower opens, remove leaves, useful trails;

Solomon's seal   1, treat after flowering;
Sweet chestnut   1, wire single leaves after treatment;
Skimma   2, useful shape;
Whitebeam   1, light on one side.

METHOD 2

Bergenia   3, very dark;
Camellia   4, glossy, dark;
Fatsia japonica   3, may need wiring, useful large leaves;
Ferns   2, pick when spores show;
Hosta   2, not always successful;
Ivy   3, larger leaves useful;
Magnolia   4, tough, dark brown;
Rubber plant   4, useful large leaf.

Drying by Hanging up

Acanthus flowers long useful stems, prickly, perennial;
Achillea flowers very tough and useful, pick when very mature, yellow
    variety best, perennial;
Allium seedheads, varying sizes, dry standing up bulb;
Amaranthus cordatus flower useful trails, annual;
Angelica seedheads, dry standing up, biennial;
Bulrush seedheads, dries standing up;
Cardoon looks like an artichoke, perennial;
Chinese lantern fruits perennial;
Delphinium, flowers keep colour well if dried quickly, perennial;
Dock seedheads, grows wild;
Globe thistle pick before flowers open, perennial;
Hogweed seedheads, biennial;
Honesty seedheads, biennial;
Hydrangea flowers dry standing in a small amount of water when
    beginning to feel papery on the plant, shrub;
Pampas grass may be stood up to dry, perennial;
Poppy seedheads, perennial;
Pussy willow catkins, dry standing up shrub;
Sea holly flowers perennial;
Straw flowers small but useful for making cones, annual;
Teasel seedheads, biennial;
Verbascum fruits, biennial.

9

Organising the Church Flowers

It is essential to have the supply and the arrangement of flowers in the church well organised so that the flower arrangers know the procedure and there is no slip up which results in a church without fresh flowers. This is not difficult and most churches already have a satisfactory system.

Flower arrangers

The flowers are often arranged by willing amateurs, either working in a team if the church is a big one or in small groups. Sometimes one person is employed to arrange all the flowers (or does them voluntarily) and professional florists are employed in some cathedrals. I feel that it is sensible to have more than one person involved because, accomplished and dedicated as she may be, other flower arrangers should also be knowledgeable and experienced in order to take over if the permanent arranger needs help or is unable to continue. Many people enjoy the opportunity of adding beauty to the church and like to feel they are helping to do so. In some churches a different person does the flowers each week. In others four people each take one Sunday a month, with another person to act as a reserve and to arrange the flowers for any fifth Sunday.

THE FLOWER ARRANGEMENT DAY

Friday or Saturday are the better days for arranging the flowers. There are plenty of them in the shops at that time and it is important that the flowers look fresh for the Sunday services. If the church is visited by many people on Saturdays then it is better to arrange the flowers on Fridays. Someone should also go into the church during the middle of the week, if it is kept open, to check the condition of the flowers. A church looks very uncared for if faded or wilted flowers are left in it.

THE FLOWER GUILD OR COMMITTEE

A guild or committee may be formed to look after the flowers. It should include any experienced flower arrangers; people who are not experienced but show interest; one or two good organisers and perhaps anyone who has facilities for growing flowers. It may be helpful to include someone who can provide transport. The guild or committee should meet sometimes to make plans for forthcoming Sundays and special events.

A SECRETARY OR CHAIRMAN. A leader with overall responsibility is necessary to see that everything runs smoothly and to take the chair at meetings. Even a small church will need a secretary or organiser to co-ordinate activities. This can be a most enjoyable and rewarding task.

Special events, including festivals, should be planned well ahead and details discussed so that the flower arrangers are well prepared. Members of local flower clubs may be invited to give additional help when required and many of their members are experienced. They are usually delighted to be asked to send a representative to any planning meetings.

Funds

There are various ways of raising funds. Many members of the congregation are happy to donate money or flowers, especially for certain dates that have significance for them; sometimes the church collection may be allocated to the flower fund; some money may be held back from the proceeds of a flower festival; coffee mornings and sales may be held, including bring-and-buy, produce and plant stalls. A box clearly marked 'Flower Fund' may be placed near the entrance to the church so that visitors who have enjoyed the flowers may make a contribution. A flower arrangement placed close to it looks attractive.

It is essential if flowers are charged to the flower fund that each arranger knows how much money she can claim. She may from choice spend more than the allowance but a 'ceiling' sum should be given so that the flower fund can be carefully budgeted to last throughout the year.

Rota

Three lists must be made at the beginning of each year, or half year, unless the flower arranging is always undertaken by one individual or a committee. A sheet of paper, headed 'Flowers', 'Date' and 'Name' should be placed in a conspicuous place so that people can fill it in. It should ask people willing to do the flowers to add their names to the list. There should also be a space for people who are willing to be called upon at short notice. It is a help to have a second list of people who may be willing to call in at the church, if it is left open during the week, to check the flowers, fill up containers with water, sweep up petals and replace dead flowers. This could be the responsibility of the person who has arranged the flowers, or it could be a willing member of the congregation who lives nearby.

A third list can be drawn up of people willing to donate flowers or the money for flowers. They may wish to do this in someone's memory or for other personal reasons. This list may be headed 'Date' and 'Donor (flowers or money for flowers)'. The arranger should know how much has been donated and also if there is any preference for the variety of flowers.

INSTRUCTIONS TO ARRANGERS

It is very helpful and saves endless repetition by the organiser if *a duplicated list of instructions* is given to each arranger. It should give details of the procedure, including when and where the flowers are arranged; any allowance given; the location of the key to the church; how to dispose of rubbish; the sources of water, containers, mechanics; the chief organiser and her deputy's addresses and telephone numbers; any special rules applicable to the church (such as if flowers are allowed on the altar); the colours of altar frontals; whether certain colours are to be used for the flowers; hints on conditioning and picking; suggestions for flowers that last well; sources of supply, such as nurserymen. It is also a good thing to suggest that flat shoes should be worn and in cold weather warm clothing. It is essential for the secretary, or organiser, to send a reminder each week to the person who has undertaken to arrange the flowers if she is not a regular arranger working in a team.

Disposal of flowers

Dead flowers should be placed in a bin provided for this purpose although some churchyards have compost heaps. When churches are kept open all week the flowers are left in place after the Sunday services. Otherwise the flowers are usually taken to sick, elderly or bereaved members of the congregation, after the Sunday evening service.

It is a pleasing gesture to include a card with a message of encouragement and perhaps a text. The organiser of the church flowers should arrange that someone delivers the flowers and that paper is available for wrapping them. The names of recipients should be recorded in a book so that the flowers are sent in turn to those who will enjoy them.

Whenever possible it is a good idea to arrange some of the flowers in foam in a plastic saucer or inexpensive container because they can then be delivered already arranged. Most recipients will appreciate this.

When the flowers are taken to hospital it also saves nurses' time if the flowers arrive arranged. Alternatively if the flowers are in the church containers they may be removed and re-arranged in foam in inexpensive containers.

The church magazine

It is helpful to have a column in the church magazine, leaflet or newsletter to give information about flowers. It can contain acknowledgements for flowers, the rota, helpful hints on conditioning and picking; a list of flowers that are needed for various weeks or for special occasions; news of festivals and possibly an article on flower arranging, the legends of flowers, how to grow them and so on.

Team work

Big churches and cathedrals may need a large team of flower arrangers and consequently more detailed organisation. The flowers may be donated and could need collection. They should otherwise be sent to the church at a specified time, preferably early on Friday morning if they are already conditioned or if not, on Thursday evening so that they can be placed in deep water overnight. The team should meet early on Friday morning, before visitors arrive, to sort the flowers into groups for the various containers and to arrange them. Each member of the team should take turns at arranging in every position so that she gets used to the different containers. Visitors are often very interested in the church flowers and it promotes good will if the arrangers can find time to answer queries.

CLASSES

Most flower arrangers benefit from classes from time to time, whether or not they are experienced. A day could be arranged with a tutor when everyone does a practical arrangement and receives kindly assessment and constructive suggestions or a demonstration could be given. A series of classes may be organised and the local flower club may be able to suggest a tutor. It is also possible to arrange a course through a college of further education. The head of the department concerned will find a flower arranging tutor and it could add to the interest to have a minister to teach subjects such as church architecture, the Church's Year and so on.

Other churches in the district may be willing to join in this project and the course of half a day a week could run for from twelve to thirty weeks. This idea has tremendous possibilities as the colleges have excellent facilities, the churches will advertise the course and, apart from the practical side of flower arranging, the course will promote understanding and friendship amongst the students of various denominations. It may also be a good idea, to stimulate interest and ideas, to take a party of flower arrangers to see other church festivals.

CHILDREN

Children love flowers and I believe it is important to teach them flower arrangement early in life. Classes are enjoyed by girls and boys who can be made responsible for the flowers in the children's corner of the church. These children may well grow up to be the church flower arrangers in future years.

The church flower cupboard

A cupboard can be equipped for flower arrangement in a convenient vestry or room, available to all those concerned with arranging flowers in the church. The leader of the group should see that the cupboard is kept tidy, well equipped and has careful, listed instructions for the care of equipment. The cupboard may include:

containers;
flower scissors, a small sharp knife;
rolls of two-inch and one-inch wire netting;
blocks of foam;
small polythene bags, sheets of polythene or dust sheets;
string and wool, stub wires and reel wire;
large pinholders, foam pinholders;
several buckets and a watering can with a long spout;
foam saucers, candlecups;
elastic bands that are strong, Sellotape;
Plasticine, Bostik strip, Oasis fix or similar compounds;
dowels and canes;
an assortment of baking tins or food tins painted a dark colour;
coarse sand;
a few heavy stones and lengths of plumbers' lead for weighting
    containers;
metal cones and tubes;
a dust pan and brush, mop and bucket, clean rag, dusters;

10

Flower Festivals

Flowers speak a universal language understood by people of every tongue in every age . . . THE DEAN OF YORK at the Festival of Flowers in York Minster, 1972

Flower festivals are inspiring occasions. All who see the flowers are uplifted and thankful for the loveliness of the earth. Many people join together to give glory to God, proclaiming him as the creator of beauty and in doing this they are united in joy and reverence.

I am quite certain that this is the most important reason for holding a church flower festival. There is also the happiness of staging a special event and the sense of achievement after it. So many people work together towards a single purpose in happy participation, and everyone gives unselfishly and devotedly of their time and energy. There are jobs for everyone and this helps lonely people to make friends, welcomes strangers and stimulates a community spirit which does so much towards creating a united and thriving church.

A flower festival attracts visitors to the church who would not otherwise have come and this does nothing but good. Finally, money may be contributed towards something that is desperately needed such as repairs to the church, central heating, a new organ or set of hymn books.

The National Association of Flower Arrangement Societies, which has many clubs throughout the British Isles and also a number of overseas associates, has been, and continues to be, responsible for thousands of cathedral and church flower festivals. It encourages a very high standard of artistic beauty and meticulous organisation. Through the efforts of flower arrangers many hundreds of thousands of pounds have been raised to repair, protect and enhance our lovely cathedrals and churches. Festivals have varied in scope from simple ones in country churches using only garden flowers to resplendent spectacles involving hundreds of flower arrangers in St Paul's Cathedral and Westminster Abbey.

Behind any successful and happy event lies careful planning. Time and thought spent in preparation are always worthwhile and the occasion runs smoothly as a result. Most people like to know exactly what, when and how they are to contribute to the event and then no one becomes ruffled and everyone gives of their best.

It is essential that from the beginning there is a happy relationship between the clergy and other church officials, the flower arrangers and other helpers. If any difficulties arise in the running of a festival it is usually because some problem has not been fully discussed from everyone's point of view. When a flower club, or more than one flower club, is asked to take part it is essential to determine the various responsibilities. The flower club may be responsible for the whole festival or only for the flower arrangements but this should be decided in the early planning stages. The position of church groups should also be determined and the church flower guild or flower arrangers must be considered. They may be made responsible for a section of the church.

Further points for the consideration of the inaugurators of the festival, even before the committee is formed, are

1. *Dates and duration of the festival* including the times of opening, staging and dismantling, taking into account the availability of flowers, holiday periods, counter attractions, winter travel.
2. *Special services* during the festival. The flower arrangers might enjoy a brief service of praise when the arrangements are completed, and certainly special services are desirable for the general public. These normally attract a large congregation. (Provision should be made for unexpected weddings and funerals during the time of the festival.)
3. *The position of the flower arrangements in the church* because the wishes of the clergy must be respected in this regard, especially for those on the altar or Communion table, the font and the pulpit. Protection of the fabric of the building, the movement of furniture and extra lighting must also be considered.
4. *Finances* including the estimated cost of staging the festival; a possible allowance for flowers; fund raising prior to the event; insurance for theft, damage, accident and bad weather; brochure selling, collecting boxes and the allocation of profits.
5. *The theme and title of the festival* which may be anyone's suggestions but should be approved by all those responsible for the festival. Special customs, local interests, the church treasure, may be included. It is important that some of the flower arrangements have a message and are not merely decorative.
6. *Publicity* because the responsibility for this can be taken on by the church authorities who may have special contacts. If not, this vital part of the festival should be in the care of someone who is knowledgeable in this field as it can make all the difference to the attendance.
7. *Printing* because the church may have special facilities for printing

leaflets, posters, tickets, directional and theme title cards.

8. *Catering* which may be undertaken by a church group, the flower club or a professional organisation. The facilities and scope of refreshments must be discussed.

9. *Helpers* such as those in organisations attached to the church, including the Flower Guild, Mothers' Union, Sunday School and Young People's groups, Guides and Scouts, Young Wives, who should be invited to take a definite part in the festival.

10. *General facilities* such as cloakrooms, parking, work and store rooms should be considered before the festival is finally inaugurated.

The committee

After these important considerations have been discussed with the church authorities, the appointed chairman should select a committee, taking the areas of responsibility into consideration. Representatives from the various groups should be included in it. It is helpful to write down the areas of responsibility and then to appoint a committee member to look after each section who can appoint a small committee of helpers outside the Festival committee. The number depends on the size and scope of the event. If clear 'terms of reference' are drawn up for each committee member, overlapping of work and omissions are normally avoided. Some suggested areas of responsibility, which could be subdivided, are

THE CHAIRMAN

Overall responsibility for the general organisation;

Liaison with the church authorities;

Co-ordination of the groups of workers, making sure that each helper knows:

details of the work required;

when to report for duty;

the length of duty;

what to bring;

what to buy and the allowance;

whether sandwiches, coffee, warm clothes, flat heels should be taken.

Chairmanship at meetings;

Selection of committee members;

Instigation of fund-raising events;

Invitations to special guests;

Keeping the vice-chairman fully informed;

Arrangements for music during the festival and possibly bell ringing;

Written records for future events;

The disposal of flowers after the festival;

Seeing that there is always a happy atmosphere amongst the workers.

SECRETARY

Correspondence and minutes of meetings;

Provision of agendas;

Letters of thanks (signed by the chairman).

TREASURER

Opening a festival account at the bank;

Drawing up a budget;

Arranging extra insurance;

Paying bills and obtaining receipts;

Receiving money and giving receipts;

Keeping a cash book and a float of petty cash;

Providing collecting boxes for the festival;

Making fund-raising suggestions;

Determining, with the committee, the extent of payment for expenses
(such as postage, telephone, travel);

Arranging an auditor;

Providing a financial report after the festival.

A simple budget includes

Expenses	*Income*
Flowers and mechanics	Gifts
Catering	Advance donations
Postage, telephone	Church collections
Travel	Brochure sales
Publicity and advertising	Catering
Printing	Fund raising events
Paid help	Special sales
Contingencies (10 per cent should be added)	(The above must be estimates based on previous experience)

FUND RAISING

Normally it is much more satisfactory to have money in hand *before the festival* to pay most of the expenses. A loan may be granted by the church authorities but this may be difficult and a better method is to raise money by running special events. The chairman of the festival will feel much happier about buying flowers and other necessities if the money is already available. Money can be raised for 'A festival flower fund' by coffee mornings, bring-and-buy stalls, cake and preserve stalls, plant sales, an evening of slides or films, a raffle or tombola and similar projects.

FESTIVAL DESIGNER

The artistic planning, including the individual themes, the position, colours, shapes of the arrangements, suggestions for types of flowers and foliage;

The briefing of flower arrangers, including visits to the church to show people where they are to work and letters confirming details and staging times;

The design and organisation of exhibits such as church treasures, fabrics, vestments, plate;

The provision of working tables and spaces, storage, and water facilities, extra lighting for dark positions;

The organisation of flowers from nurseries, the congregation and other donors, bulk buying;

Conditioning of plant material received from sources other than individual flower arrangers;

The use of the church flower arrangement containers;

Viewing, staging and dismantling times for the arrangers;

The protection of furnishings and floors;

The movement of furniture (with the church authorities' permission);

The use of nails and screws (only with permission);

The attendance of a carpenter and electrician if necessary (through the church authorities);

The provision of step ladders;

The provision of staging materials including:

watering cans;
pins, nails, screws;
tools such as a hammer, screwdriver, scissors;
polythene sheeting;
stub wire, reel wire, string, Sellotape;
Oasis and Oasis fix, Plasticine, glue;
tubes and canes;
pen and paper.

PUBLICITY CHAIRMAN

The distribution of handbills and posters;
Writing of press releases;
Television, radio and newspaper coverage;
Magazine coverage, including parish magazines and other church publications;
Entry in the publication *The Flower Arranger*, 'Dates for your Diary' section if a flower club is involved;
Banners and car stickers, if used;
Press preview arrangements, if any;
Provision of photographs for the press or arrangements for the press to take photographs, photography for a set of slides;
Publicity to other organisations such as other churches, Women's Institutes, Townswomen's Guilds, Flower Clubs;
Shop window displays;
Advertisements (paid);
Road signs (AA or RAC);
Lists of people to be specially invited to a preview or dedication service;
Collection of press cuttings for future help.

PRESS RELEASE. A press release should be double-spaced, simple and quick to read.
It should include:

A 'headline' title, to attract attention;
The title of the festival if different from the headline;
The venue;
Dates and times of opening;
Parking and refreshment facilities;
Special features of the festival;
Financial aim;
Flower club name, and sometimes the artistic designer;
The publicity officer's name, address and telephone number for further information.

HANDBILLS AND POSTERS. These should include the same information but condensed and well spaced for rapid reading, using different sizes of print.

PRINTING CHAIRMAN

Printing of handbills, posters, car stickers (printing time may be booked ahead);

Collating and printing of the brochure;

Provision of stewards' badges;

Printing of title cards for flower arrangements (in conjunction with the artistic designer);

Printing of the direction cards, such as 'exit' (in conjunction with the committee member in charge of stewarding);

Printing of tickets for any special services.

STEWARD'S CHAIRMAN

Organisation of the viewing route, including doors to be kept shut or open, provision of ropes and stands;

Placement of direction signs;

Selling of brochures;

Compiling a stewards' rota;

Car parking arrangements and attendants' rota;

Police notification;

First Aid (the Red Cross or the St John's Ambulance Brigade may be able to attend for the festival), Elastoplast and simple first aid equipment at staging time;

Assistance to arrangers when unloading;

Arrangement of cloakroom facilities, including soap and towels;

Provision of extra buckets for flowers, some dust sheets;

Provision of large polythene bags or boxes for rubbish and the disposal of rubbish;

Cleaning materials, including brushes and pan, mop and bucket, cloths and dusters;

Provision of heating if necessary;

Topping up of flower arrangement containers with water through the festival and replacement of flowers;

Seeing that flower arrangements and accessories are not handled by the public;

Arranging for photography with the publicity committee member;

Answering questions from the general public;

Keeping an eye on the money boxes;

Arranging car badges for the committee and helpers in large festivals in crowded cities, and the staggering of the arrival of cars;

Welcoming visitors.

CATERING CHAIRMAN

Deciding the extent of catering for the public and helpers, such as:

light lunches;

snacks;

tea or coffee and biscuits;
afternoon tea;
hot soup;
The charges to the public and to helpers;
Ordering and preparation of food;
Refreshment helpers' rota;
Collection of tablecloths, cutlery, china, napkins;
Provision of tables and chairs for serving food and for guests;
The table flowers;
Meals for special guests;
Provision of a board showing meal prices;
Washing-up arrangements;
Disposal of surplus food.

Designing and preparation of festivals

A church flower festival needs considerable thought with regard to design. It should not be an over-done flower show that exchanges the marquee or hall for the church. Nothing looks worse than an over-decorated effect, with flowers hiding the beautiful fabric and furnishings of the church itself. The object of the overall design should be to draw attention to the church's own beauty and not to hide or detract from it in any way. It is therefore essential to plan the position of the arrangements very carefully remembering that restraint and dignity are essential. Usually a few concentrated groups with restful spacing in between them are successful.

The use of only the most dignified and appropriate accessories is desirable. Drapes do little to enhance either the flower arrangements or the church. Why hang yards of coloured fabric over beautiful mellow stone walls that in themselves provide the most beautiful background for flowers? Bases too should be used with discretion as the natural stonework or weathered wood of the church is often more attractive than anything else. Uniform ranks of pedestals or large triangles on every window sill are not always the most beautiful way of showing flowers. It is often better if each arrangement is unique in size, colour and shape.

One should learn when to stop adding to an arrangement. The simplest flower or leaf has a world of delight in it when arranged with skill and imagination. F. W. Burbidge in *Domestic Floriculture*, published as a second edition in 1875, writes

'... we use flowers and fruits to give an idea of God's bounty and providential goodness and the more simple our arrangements are, the more likely is this end to be attained.'

The flowers in the Poets' Corner of Westminster Abbey complementing the monument. By courtesy of NAFAS

Sometimes one type of plant material such as a bowl of one variety of rose with foliage, or a mass of gladioli in one colour, is more striking and meaningful than a mixed flower arrangement. Think of the loveliness of a drift of bluebells in the country, forget-me-nots by a stream, or the nodding heads of a mass of daffodils in the spring.

A variety of shapes and sizes can be selected for the arrangements, always being sure that the shape suits the position for which it is in-

Flowers arranged in a corner of the church at Lyme Hall, Disley, by Dorothy Haworth. By courtesy of Amateur Gardening

tended in the church. Full use can be made of any special features so that attention is drawn to them by means of the arrangements.

COLOUR HARMONIES

In a small church an overall colour harmony is often the best. One colour used in variety can be very effective. A deep shade may be used for one end of the church, gradually lightening to the other end.

Green is often neglected although much used by our ancestors. It is delightful seen against stone walls and columns, especially in garlands without flowers, or with flowers added in one colour. Growing plants are always lovely and may be massed in groups. There are many greens and textures to give variety and interest. The plants may be borrowed or, given enough time, specially grown for the festival.

The Glory of Lebanon shall come to you, the cypress, the plane and the pine, to beautify the place of my sanctuary

ISAIAH 60: 13

The colours of stone, wood, carpets, curtains, cushions, faded coats of arms, glass and silver, rows of hymn books, vestments, the altar frontal in use at the time of the festival, should all be considered when the flower colours are chosen.

Flower arrangements that are adjacent to each other should be in gentle harmony, with a gradual change to make it appear more restful. The time of year also affects the choice as some colours seem more suitable in different seasons, such as oranges and reds when it is cold, yellow in the spring.

Stained glass windows are normally colourful and it can sometimes be a mistake to pick out every colour in the flower arrangement. The choice of only one of the colours for the flowers might be more effective.

When themes are interpreted thought should be given to the colour which has many associations for people both in life generally and also as used by the church. The following are the generally accepted interpretations of the significance of colours, as used by the Church:

Black	Solemnity, negation, sickness, death;
Black and white	Humility, purity of life;
Blue	Heavenly love, unveiling of truth. Traditional colour of St Mary, the Blessed Virgin. In the English Scheme of Liturgical Colours, blue is used in Advent and on the Pre-Lenten 'Gesima Sundays';
Brown	Renunciation of the world, spiritual death and degradation;
Gold	See white;

5. A paschal candle decorated with spring flowers by Ruth Townley in St Mary's Church, Goring-by-Sea

6. Flowers for a festival on the font of St Wilfrid's Parish Church, Mobberley, Cheshire, arranged by Jean Taylor

7. 'Farming in the Past' arranged by Joyce Manaton in the Parish Church of St Buryan. Simple flowers are used with a stone trough and grain crusher. By courtesy of Richard L. Jeffery

8. Foliage arranged by Sheila Macqueen at the High Altar in Westminster Abbey. By courtesy of NAFAS.

Green	Spring, triumph of life over death, charity, regeneration of soul through good works, hope. Epiphany and Trinity seasons;
Grey	Ashes, humility, mourning;
Purple	Royalty, imperial power (God the Father);
Red	Martyred saints, love, hate, sovereign power. Pentecost;
Violet	Love, truth, passion, suffering. In the western use, Advent and Lent;
White (Gold)	Innocence of soul, purity, holiness of life. Christmas, The Epiphany, Easter, The Ascension, Trinity Sunday, the Transfiguration, All Saints;
Yellow	Dingy: Infernal light, degradation, jealousy, treason, deceit.

Religious Orders are sometimes represented by the colours of their habits:

Black	The Benedictines, Augustinians, Jesuits, Cowley Fathers;
Grey	The Franciscans. Dark brown if the reformed branch;
White	The reformed branch of the Benedictines, Cistercians, Praemonstratensians, the Order of the Holy Cross;
Black over white	The Dominicans;
White over brown	The Carmelites;

(Taken from *Saints, Signs and Symbols* by W. Ellwood Post, published S.P.C.K.)

DETAILED PREPARATION FOR THE DESIGNER

Obtain a scale plan of the church;

Walk around the church looking for suitable places for flowers;

Mark in any special features and the viewing route, as these concern the positioning of the arrangements;

Mark on the map the position of the intended arrangements. In a cathedral or large church these may be grouped under a group leader. Colour coding using small different coloured circles for each group is helpful. The same colour should be used on the plan, correspondence, boxes, buckets and so on.

Every flower arranger should see the setting for the arrangement and discuss the design with the festival designer. When personal viewing is impossible, because of long distance travel, then a sketch of the position should be sent.

Organise special lighting where necessary, remember that flowers do not show when seen against a light such as in front of a window.

Every flower arranger should receive a letter containing these details:
the theme of the festival and historical notes on the church,
the theme of the arrangement.
the accessories, if any, to be used,
a general idea of the shape and colouring,
the size of the intended arrangement,
the allowance for flowers (a ceiling must be given),
whether any flowers will be available through bulk buying,
the dates for viewing the church beforehand, for staging and for dismantling.

THEMES

Some of the flower arrangements should be more than simply decorative because if so, the designs can become a means of communication, and can help a visitor to the church to absorb a deeper knowledge of Christian teachings. There are many ideas for interpretation and the minister of the church will have suggestions and will be able to give guidance.

Themes can also interpret the life of the town, the history of the church and the life of people buried or remembered in it. Other festivals can be combined with a flower festival, such as a Saints' Day, Easter, Whitsun, Harvest, Christmas, Mothering Sunday, local festivals such as the tulip festivals in the fen country.

Tributes may be made to ecclesiastical craftsmen, to writers, musicians and famous men. Works of art, paintings, carvings, sculpture can be borrowed from local people, galleries, universities and museums to combine with flowers. Thomas Campbell wrote of daisies and buttercups, Alfred Tennyson of roses and lilies, Wordsworth of daffodils, William Blake of wild flowers, Milton of 'herbs, fruit and flowers glistening with dew', Longfellow of 'tremulous leaves with soft silver lining'.

The designer must do some homework on possible themes to give ideas to the arrangers. They can then follow these up with more detailed research. Gimmickry and inartistic accessories should be avoided and the designer should suggest suitable ways of interpreting themes to those who have not used flowers in this manner. For example, 'They shall lay hands on the sick and they shall recover' (Mark 16. 18) could include herbs and a cruse of Holy oil used in anointing the sick. If possible the most experienced flower arrangers should be used for this aspect of the festival. The less experienced will be happy to help with garlands and large-scale arrangements under the guidance of more advanced flower arrangers.

The Calendar of the Church makes an excellent theme and title.

110

Included should be the season of Advent, Christmas, Epiphany, the season of Lent, Easter, the Festival of the Ascension, Whitsuntide, the Feast of Holy Trinity. See *The Christian Calendar*, published by Weidenfeld and Nicolson, for further help. Flower arrangers should consult the minister of the church with regard to appropriate texts and colours.

Ember Days	Ordination of Priests
Holy Communion	Maundy Thursday
Baptism	The Holy Bible
All Saints	Remembrance Sunday
Ash Wednesday	Mothering Sunday
Consecration of Bishops	Confirmation
Evening prayer	Morning prayer
Holy Innocents' Day	Good Friday
Matrimony	Plough Sunday

The Patron Saints make interesting interpretations in flowers:

St Agnes (21 January)	Betrothed couples, gardeners and maidens
St Ambrose (7 December)	Beekeepers and domestic animals
St Andrew (30 November)	Scotland, fishermen and sailors
St Anthony (17 January)	Lost things
St Augustine (28 August)	Theologians
St Barbara (4 December)	Builders and firework makers
St Benedict (21 March)	Coppersmiths and schoolboys
St Bernard of Clairvaux (20 August)	Beekeepers
St Boniface (5 June)	Brewers and tailors
St Catherine (25 November)	Philosophers and spinsters
St Cecilia (22 November)	Musicians
St Christopher (25 July)	Sailors and travellers
St Cornelius (16 September)	Cattle and domestic animals
St Cuthbert (20 March)	Shepherds and seafarers
St David (1 March)	Wales
St Dorothy (6 February)	Brides and gardeners
St Dunstan (19 May)	Blacksmiths, goldsmiths and the blind
St Eligius (1 December)	Smiths and metal workers
St Elisabeth of Hungary (19 November)	Bakers and beggars
St Francis (4 October)	Animals
St Gabriel (Archangel (24 March)	Postmen
St George (23 April)	England, cavalrymen, chivalry and soldiers
St Giles (1 September)	Beggars, blacksmiths and cripples

St Gregory the Great (12 March)	Musicians
St Jerome (30 September)	Students
St John the Evangelist (27 September)	Booksellers, painters, printers and publishers
St Joseph (19 March)	Carpenters, engineers and the family
St Jude (28 October)	The desperate
St Lawrence (10 August)	Cooks, cutters, armouries and schoolboys
St Luke (18 October)	Doctors, goldsmiths and sculptors
St Margaret (20 July)	Women (especially maidens), nurses and peasants
St Mark (25 April)	Venice, glaziers and notaries
St Martin of Tours (11 November)	Beggars, innkeepers and tailors
St Matthew (21 September)	Bankers and tax collectors
St Michael, Archangel (29 September)	Artists and soldiers
St Nicholas (6 December)	Children and captives
St Patrick (17 March)	Ireland
St Paul (30 June)	Musicians
St Peter (29 June)	Bakers, butchers and clockmakers
St Raphael, Archangel (24 October)	Guardian angels
St Sebastian (20 January)	Armourers, ironmongers and potters
St Teresa of Avila (15 October)	Those in need of grace
St Thomas (21 December)	Architects, carpenters and geometricians
St Ursula (21 October)	Maidens, drapers and teachers
St Zita (27 April)	Domestic servants

Effective festivals can be planned around ecclesiastical embroidery, 'All things bright and beautiful', The *Benedicite*, the Parables, the Psalms, texts from the Bible, such as:

'I am the light of the world', John 8.12

'I am the good Shepherd', John 10.11

'Lo I am with you even unto the end of the world', Matthew 28.20

'Suffer little children to come unto me', Luke 18.16

'This is my body. This is my blood', Matthew 26.26 (for the Sacrament)

'Go ye into the world and preach the gospel to every creature', Mark 16.15

'Consider the lilies', Luke 12.27

'Man shall not live by bread alone', Luke 4.4

'Peace, be still', Mark 4.39

'If any man will come after me let him deny himself and take up his cross and follow me', Mattew 16.24 (depicting monastery life)
'He that believeth and is baptised shall be saved', Mark 10.16
'Greater love hath no man', John 15.13

Hymns and carols can also be interpreted, work in other lands, appropriate poetry and prose, the Sermon on the Mount with ten main themes:

the poor	the pure
the sorrowful	the peacemakers
the gentle	the persecuted
the righteous	the salt of the earth
the merciful	the light of the world

and the life of the Blessed Virgin Mary:

the nativity of the Virgin Mary	the Purification
the Visitation	the Epiphany
the Annunciation	the Passover at Jerusalem
the Conception	the Marriage at Cana
the Birth of Jesus	the Crucifixion

THE BROCHURE

The brochure needs considerable thought and planning. It will be taken home by visitors and re-read and therefore it seems important that it should include more than factual information. It could include:

a message from the minister,
a history of the church,
a plan of the church,
articles of local interest,
a list of the arrangements, numbered in order of viewing (to correspond with a number on the arrangement and on the plan),
appropriate texts,
details of the themes interpreted,
photography and drawings.

Other information to include is the name of the church, flower club, committee, dates and times of the festival, church service times, how the money made will be used, organisations that have given help, the thanks of the chairman, advertisements.

The cover should be attractive to encourage sales. Printing such a booklet can be expensive and the total cost should be gone into carefully, as it is important that the profits made in selling the brochure do not exceed the printing costs. A careful balance of content, type of paper, size and so on must be considered.

The Font

The font is a favourite place for flowers at a festival but the minister should be consulted before they are placed *in* the cavity. If he does not mind then it makes a lovely container. It is normally large but can be

'*The Descent of the Holy Spirit in Baptism' interpreted by Phyllis MacGregor with white feathers and chrysanthemums at Deganwy Church*

reduced by standing a smaller bowl inside, raised on a block. Alternatively a circle of wood may be used as a lid and flowers arranged in a large bowl on top.

When neither cavity or lid may be used flowers may be garlanded around the top, remembering to leave room for the minister's hand to reach the water if there is a christening. Flowers could also encircle the base or the stem, or a spray could be arranged on one side.

'It is better to decorate too little than too much. The latter is a constant error fallen into when there are so many willing hands to help and all are eager to produce some new and dazzling effect that may give additional glory to their particular church. It may seem unnecessary to carry out rules for what is intended for an ornament for so short a time, but whatever is attempted is worth doing well: and in performing this work it should be remembered that it is not desired as a display of personal skill but is undertaken to impress upon the minds and hearts of all beholders rejoicing over an event of great importance to them, which is most surely done by presenting to them a complete whole, where architecture and decorations go hand in hand, than in attracting their attention by fantastic or gorgeous devices.'

From a review of Church Festival Decorations in the magazine *The Garden*, 11 December 1880. Contributed by Mary Pope, the Founder President of The National Association of Flower Arrangement Societies (NAFAS).

11

Special Effects

For festivals and other special occasions flowers can be arranged in unusual ways to decorate churches and cathedrals. This arouses excitement and comment and attracts people to the festival. Special effects can be made in the form of cone-shaped designs, garlands, swags and

A garland designed by Irene Mottershead to complement the carvings on the pulpit of St James Church, Birkdale. Honesty leaves were glued to the brackets from which hung garlands made with polythene and foam. Courtesy of H. Leadbetter

plaques. They are not difficult to make once you know the mechanics, but these are different from the supports normally used for flowers.

Cones are thought to have been a form of flower decoration in Byzantium, a Greek city in the fourth century. They were fashioned by binding stems to a central stick and are still made this way in Mexico. Garlands are an even more ancient form of flower decoration and were popular in classical Greece and Rome. Some of the loveliest garlands of fruit, foliage and flowers can be seen in Renaissance paintings and the garlands of the della Robbia family have been widely copied. In the late seventeenth century Grinling Gibbons carved exquisite garlands and swags of fruit and flowers in wood and these may still be seen in British country houses and are a great source of inspiration to modern flower arrangers. Perhaps we do not make enough of this type of decoration nowadays, probably because they take time, but they are very lovely for special occasions and well worth a little patience. Two or three flower arrangers can make a cone or a garland together and enjoy doing it.

Cones

METHOD 1. A simple cone may be made by standing a soaked block of foam upright in a container, secured by a foam pinholder. The corners of the top of the block should be sliced off to give the cone shape. Cover the

Making a cone with foam

Method 1

block with leaves placed as flat as possible against the foam to conceal it. Flowers, and fruit on small sticks (such as cocktail sticks) can be added afterwards. Single chrysanthemums or similar flowers are the most successful as they lie flat and fill the cone quickly so that fewer flowers are needed. Small fruits look decorative. Plums, apricots, grapes, tiny peppers, apples, tomatoes, pine cones and nuts are some of the fruits that may be used to give a rich and colourful effect.

METHOD 2. A larger cone can be made using a wire-netting foundation. Cut a triangle with a slightly curved base from one-inch-mesh wire netting. Twist the cut ends together on the long sides to make a cone, remembering that the plant material will extend from the wire netting

Wire netting cone

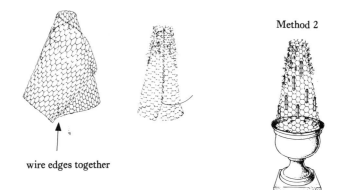

Method 2

wire edges together

and that a slim foundation will look a lot wider when completed. Fill the cone with pieces of soaked foam or damp moss. Insert sprigs of foliage to cover the netting and then add flowers, and fruit on sticks, if desired. When moss is used as a filling small tubes may be inserted to hold flowers that need more water than can be provided by damp moss. Or a sausage of polythene holding foam may be wound, as a garland, round the foliage foundation and filled with flowers.

A cone looks better if it is placed on a container and a garden urn with a stem is suitable because it lifts the cone up and lightens the otherwise solid effect. To prevent the foam or moss from falling out of the netting a round tray, board or plate may be placed over the cavity of the container before setting the cone on the top. When a cone larger than about three feet is constructed it is advisable to give it a strong support in the centre. A broom stick is suitable and this may be set in concrete or plaster of Paris in an empty tin or plastic bucket. Knock a nail into the top of the broomstick, place the cone over the top and wire the top of the netting to the nail. Put the cone on its side on the floor to fill it with foam or moss and use wire netting to hold in the filling at the bottom of the cone. Two sticks placed crossways through the netting will give extra support. If the broomstick shows it can be painted brown or green.

METHOD 3. An easily available saucepan stand makes a good foundation for a large cone. Place blocks of foam in dishes or black painted plant saucers on each tier. Metal cones on sticks can be placed in the top to

Other mechanics for cones

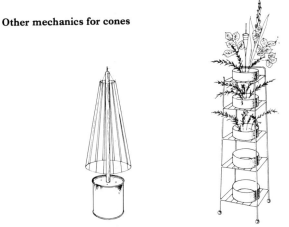

Method 4 lampshade frame   Method 3 saucepan stand

hold flowers to give greater height and a tapered appearance. Long-stemmed plant material should be inserted to conceal the framework. This foundation makes a rather looser looking cone. It can be given more height when placed on a plinth or an upturned, covered box.

METHOD 4. A smaller cone can be made using a lampshade frame as a foundation. Cone-shaped frames are available and may be lined with polythene filled with foam or moss, kept in by a circle of wire netting attached to the bottom. Alternatively the lampshade frame may be completely covered with netting and then filled.

METHOD 5. Cones made of a type of plastic foam for dried plant material are available at florists and flower clubs. Stems can be pushed into the foam very quickly. These cones are usually not more than eight to twelve inches high and for a larger design blocks of dry Oasis should be used, constructing the cone by any of the suggested methods.

DESIGN

It is normally better to begin by covering with foliage. Small-leafed foliage such as box, cupressus, yew lasts well and the woody stems go in easily. This conceals the foundation and is more economical than trying to cover it with flowers and fruit. These can be added afterwards over

119

the foliage. Cover the cone entirely with fruit and flowers or place in random small groups in concentric circles or in a spiral.

Flowers placed in various designs

Garlands

Garlands of fruit, flowers and foliage are delightful and give a very festive air. They may gracefully adorn pillars, fonts, statues and pulpits and form decorative edgings for tables, pews and choir stalls. There are several ways of making them. If stored in polythene bags in a cool place they may be made a week ahead. Flowers may be added nearer the time.

METHOD 1. Cut a strip of thin polythene about 6 inches wide and the required length. Stitch the sides together with $\frac{3}{4}$ inch margin, using a

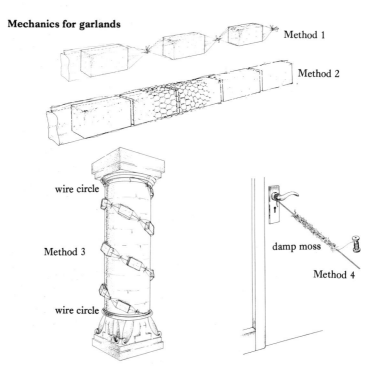

Mechanics for garlands

Method 1

Method 2

wire circle

Method 3

wire circle

damp moss

Method 4

long stitch on a sewing machine or backstitch if sewn by hand or buy
when possible a length of tube polythene. Fill this with pieces of soaked
foam leaving a 2- or 3-inch gap between each piece. Twist a short length
of reel wire tightly around the polythene in the centre of each gap so that
the tube looks like a string of sausages. This makes the garland flexible
when it is strung around a curved pillar or statue. If the foam blocks are
placed end to end without these gaps the results is a stiff garland which
is difficult to bend. Cover the tube with foliage, using if possible woody

*A simple garland on heavy wire of cupressus and white chrysanthemums
designed by Bill Lomas in St Wilfrid's Church, Mobberley*

121

stems that are easy to push through the polythene. A hole may be made, using a skewer, for softer stems. Garlands made entirely of foliage, in various shades of green with several textures, are very effective especially when encircling cream stone pillars, but flowers and fruit may be added. Most of the plant material should be placed into the tube before it is hung up, especially at the top which is hard to reach. One side should be left empty so that it will lie flat against the pillar or statue. Use wire to fix the top and bottom of the garland to a nail, or to anything suitable. Fill in any gaps once the garland is in position.

METHOD 2. Garlands may be made similarly without gaps between the blocks of foam. A strip of wire netting in one-inch mesh may be placed over the polythene to give extra support and the edges wired together. This is a good foundation for a stiffer garland that can be used as a foundation for a decorative border or edging on a railing, pew or screen. It can also be wound around a stake for a modern effect.

METHOD 3. An easy way to make garlands for a pillar is to use longlasting evergreens on a heavy wire. First place a circle of wire around the narrowest part at the top of the pillar and then similarly place a second one at the bottom. Measure a length of wire that will wind around the pillar from top to bottom making one, two or three loops around it. Thread this on to six or more small blocks of foam wrapped in thin polythene, spacing them about two feet apart, for flowers. Attach this long wire to the circle at the top, pull it tightly around the pillar and attach it to the bottom circle of wire. Add flowers and foliage to each block of polythene and place sprigs of longlasting foliage underneath the wire and next to the pillar. Fussy foliage such as cupressus will conceal the wire and last well for several days.

METHOD 4. A simple garland of longlasting evergreens may be made by binding them (using reel wire) to a rope or heavy wire. It is easier to make if one end of the rope is tied to something heavy so that it can be pulled taut as the evergreens are bound on. All foliage should face the same direction so that each stem is covered by the leaves of the sprig before. Some moisture can be provided if the rope or wire is bound with damp moss using reel wire. Insert stems into the moss. This makes a thicker garland.

METHOD 5. A garland effect at floor level may be achieved by the use of plastic troughing (made for house roofs). Fill this with foam, water or moss and add flowers and leaves.

A trough of flowers arranged by members of the church at the foot of the choir stalls in St Wilfrid's Parish Church, Mobberley

Swags

A swag is a decoration to hang up that normally shows no background or mounting. It is very effective used high on a church wall where everyone can see it easily. Often there are existing nails, screws or brackets on which a swag can be hung, but permission should be requested to knock in nails. It is a pity to damage the fabric of the church in any way and it is better to make every effort not to bang in new nails.

METHOD 1. A swag of fresh plant material may be made in foam or damp moss wrapped in polythene to conserve the moisture. The water content makes this a heavy decoration and as it is to be hung up it is advisable to use only a small block of foam. Long stems can be inserted to make a large swag. Place the foam or moss in a thin polythene bag and

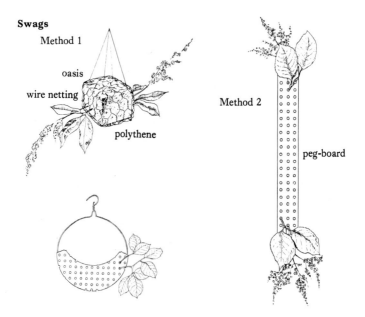

Swags

Method 1

oasis

wire netting

polythene

Method 2

peg-board

tie it up, cutting off any surplus. Cover the bag with wire netting in one-inch mesh, wiring the cut ends together. This gives extra support and also provides a means of hanging up the swag. Attach two long lengths of reel wire to the wire netting towards the back. Later when the swag is completed the other ends of these wires can be wound round a nail in the wall. Insert flower and leaf stems into the foam through the wire netting and polythene. It is easier to do this if the block is placed on the edge of a table so that the stems can flow downwards. First cover the block with leaves placed flat against the wire netting to conceal it. Then add longer stems and flowers but not on the underside of the block or water will drip out of the holes, probably on to someone's best hat! Fruit on small sticks may be used but tends to make the swag heavy. If dried plant

A swag of dried plant material in dry moss and wire arranged by Mrs E. Hustwit in York Minster

125

material is used in dry foam it will be much lighter. Wire netting is still necessary but not polythene. A swag made in a similar way looks lovely on a pew end for a festival or wedding. Hang it by means of a wire loop.

METHOD 2. A dried swag can be made for an almost permanent decoration by the previous method or cut pegboard to a desired shape and attach dried plant material by wiring it on through the holes in the peg board. Glue such as Uhu may also be used to attach lighter weight plant material. A Grinling Gibbons type swag can be made by this method and looks decorative if it includes seedheads, dried fruits, pine cones, dried flowers. There is no need for such a swag to be made only in browns as there are many subtle and beautiful colours in dried plant material. Very long, slim swags for pillars may be made on narrow pegboard.

Plaques

Plaques are hanging decorations mounted on a background that is visible and part of the design. In a church a plaque can look rather artificial and superfluous because the walls and furnishings themselves make a lovely backing for flowers. However there may be an occasion when a plaque is fitting, for example one could be made to look like a shield or coat of arms to follow a theme in a festival.

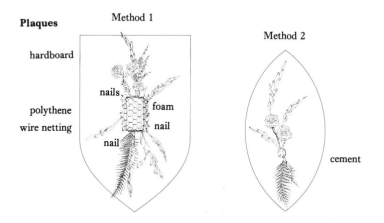

THE BACKING

Cut a piece of hardboard to the required shape. A DIY shop may do this for you if given a paper pattern or exact measurements. Paint the hardboard with emulsion paint in a soft colour chosen to set off the flowers rather than compete with them. A matt surface is better than a glossy one for the same reason. A backing may also be made of pegboard cut to shape and covered with fabric to hide the holes. A matt-textured fabric such as felt in a dull colour is normally better than a shiny fabric. The covering can be glued to the underside of the hardboard or pegboard.

METHOD 1 FOR FRESH PLANT MATERIAL. Hammer 4 nails into the hardboard, in a square near the centre. This is unnecessary for pegboard. Wrap a block of foam first in thin polythene and then in one-inch-mesh wire netting. Attach it to the nails with reel wire twisted into the netting. If pegboard is used, attach 4 lengths of reel wire to the netting and put them through the fabric and the pegboard holes, twisting them together on the underside. Insert the stems of plant material through the polythene into the foam.

METHOD 2 FOR DRIED PLANT MATERIAL. The same method can be used for dried plant material omitting the polythene and using foam. Alternatively glue may be used to attach lightweight dried seedheads, leaves and flowers to the backing. A pile of cement that takes about half an hour to dry can be squeezed on to the backing. Stems are inserted into the cement, but remember that once it has set the design is permanent. Uhu or any other clear quick-setting adhesive can also be used to stick individual pieces of plant material (normally with short stems), to the backing. Heavy plant material such as some dried seedheads should be wired through a pegboard backing for safety.

DESIGN

When making swags and plaques the same design principles should be considered as for flower arrangements. There should be a variety of shapes, and textures, one or more centres of interest to emphasise parts of the design and good spacing. It is better to cover the mechanics with leaves *before* inserting longer stems and flowers. When a background is used, as in a plaque, it is better not to let the plant material extend beyond the backing so that the arrangement is framed.

Other hanging arrangements

HANGING BASKET

When it is possible to hang a decoration freely in space without a backing wall, a hanging basket is delightful. The well known type used in porches and verandahs in summer makes a good foundation and the

A hanging basket arranged over the entrance to St Wilfrid's Parish Church, Mobberley

wire framework can be concealed with plant material. Line the basket with polythene and fill with damp moss or foam, remembering that the latter is much heavier and may be more risky to hang up. Decorative baskets may also be used, with an inner container holding water-retaining moss or soaked foam. This container should be wired into the basket for safety. A block of foam or moss wrapped in polythene and wire netting may also be used without a container. It can be suspended in the same way as a basket. This style is effective at Christmas for evergreens and holly. Remember not to make holes in the bottom near the centre or water will drip down.

COAT-HANGER DECORATION

A wire coat-hanger can be pulled into a circular shape and bound, using reel wire, with damp moss. Sprigs of foliage and small flowers can be inserted into the moss which may be covered with thin polythene to con-

Arrangements to hang up

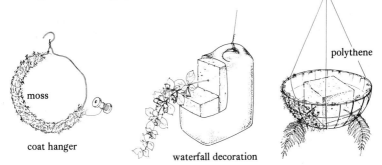

moss

coat hanger

polythene

waterfall decoration

serve moisture. If covered with plant material on both sides the circle can be free-hanging, using the coat hanger hook to suspend it. Alternatively it can be used flat against a wall. Small leafed foliage such as box is most successful.

WATERFALL DECORATION

Cut away part of a half- or one-gallon detergent container and put one to one and a half blocks of foam in the remaining cavity. Hang it up by twisting wire on the handle. Arrange flowers to spill from it.

DESIGN

In all hanging decorations plant material should be arranged so that it can be seen from all angles and looks pleasing from below. Trails of such plants as ivy or honeysuckle soften the appearance and little plant material is necessary at the centre of the design except to cover the mechanics.

A topiary tree

This is a formal decoration, like a clipped bay tree, but it is very decorative for special festivals and weddings. Various sizes may be

129

made, using the same method of construction. The following one is from 2 to 3 feet high. Hammer a 2-inch, flatheaded nail partially into the top of a 16-inch length of broom handle (from an ironmonger). Secure the other end in a plastic plant pot (without a hole) about 5–6 inches in diameter, using plaster of Paris. This is obtained from a chemist and is a white powder that sets in a few minutes when mixed with cold water. Pour the powder into the plant pot, almost to the top, and add water, stirring as you do so. When it is the consistency of thick cream, place the 'stem' into the centre and hold it in position until the plaster sets. The plastic plant pot may later be placed in a decorative outer pot but plaster should *not* be mixed in a breakable pot because it will crack.

Place half a large block of foam on the nail at the top of the stem, or alternatively use a ball of damp moss, wrapped in netting. Fill this with sprigs of foliage and flowers and fruit if desired. The stem should be painted brown or dark green and long ribbons may be added below the foliage. This decoration may be made ahead of an event if the foliage ball is wrapped in thin polythene and kept in a cool, dimly lit place. Flowers and fruit may be added nearer the time.

When larger sizes of topiary trees are made they are inclined to topple over unless the container is a heavy one. Stones, bricks or sand can add weight. When a large foliage ball is made, extra support may be given by adding two lengths of wood across the top, and through the main stem,

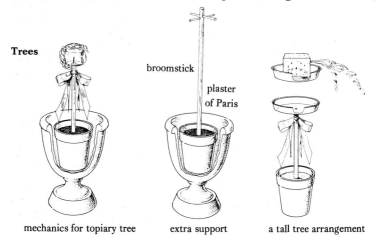

Trees

broomstick

plaster of Paris

mechanics for topiary tree   extra support   a tall tree arrangement

on which the ball can rest. They will be concealed by the foliage. A more formal effect is obtained if the foliage is clipped evenly like a football but the same basic mechanics can be used for a design with stems of varying length.

A tall tree arrangement

Using a similar base to that of the topiary tree, screw a pie tin on top of the broomstick. Place a second similar tin inside to provide a watertight container. Arrange flowers and leaves in a branching effect.

A tree arrangement of pink and yellow carnations with pink lilies designed by Molly Duerr for a wedding

A decoration for sloping window sill

Many churches have window sills which slope downwards making it difficult to stand a container on them. Foam has made it possible to decorate these with a flower arrangement. Place a block of foam in thin polythene and wire netting. Attach two lengths of wire to the top of the netting on either side at the back and twist the other ends around the metal on the window or around an unobtrusive nail.

Concealed containers

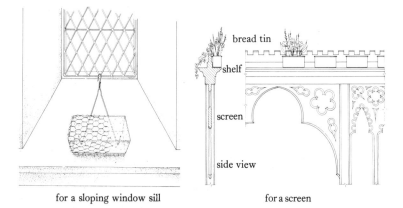

for a sloping window sill   for a screen

A decoration for the top of a screen

A screen or ledge that is wide enough at the top to take a container can be decorated very effectively if you are willing to go up a long ladder. Place a loaf tin holding foam on the ledge and wire it in place, using reel wire, so that it cannot fall off. Add plant material which trails down over the front of the screen but few flowers and leaves are needed at the top. This is a lovely decoration that can be seen by everyone in the church and it takes little plant material.

The pulpit

Often the pulpit is beautifully carved and a flower decoration is superfluous but there are occasions when it may be specially dressed up.

METHOD 1. Cover the pulpit front with a sheet of polythene and then with dark green felt attached to a hook at each corner at the back of the pulpit. Cover the felt with one-inch-mesh wire netting. Insert sprigs of longlasting foliage into the wire and add small tubes to hold water and flowers at intervals.

'The Ascension', a well-designed grouping on the screen of St Wilfrid's Parish Church, Mobberley arranged by members of the Bramhall, Hale and Wilmslow Flower Clubs

133

METHOD 2. Use lengths of aluminium strip $\frac{3}{4}$ inch by $\frac{3}{32}$ inch, drilling holes in the strip to take $\frac{3}{16}$ inch bolts at regular intervals, for securing containers. Drill two similar holes in one side of loaf tins, and bolt the containers to the strip. This can then be placed around the pulpit at any height, fastened to small hooks inside the pulpit with wire through the holes drilled in the strip. Aluminium strip is easily bent around wood and stone so this method may also be used to decorate pillars. Place the strip around the pillar and secure the ends with a bolt placed through holes in each end. Foam or crumpled wire netting can be placed in the loaf tins to hold flower arrangements.

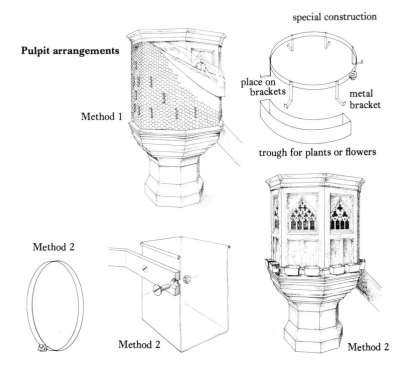

special construction

Pulpit arrangements

Method 1

place on brackets

metal bracket

trough for plants or flowers

Method 2

Method 2

Method 2

Many variations of these basic designs, using foam and moss, wire netting and polythene, can be made specifically for a church, to suit the available space and the existing furnishings. Local craftsmen can make special constructions of metal or wood to fit such places as the top of a font, the pulpit, the lectern, the foot of the choir stalls. These constructions are 'custom-built' and brought out from storage for special festivals.

134

Certain considerations should always be regarded:

1. *Stability* is essential so that a decoration never falls over. This can be achieved by using a heavy base at floor level so that it is not top heavy; by wiring designs to furnishings that are built in, such as pews; by making sure that hooks and nails can bear the weight of heavy water-filled foam. Nylon fishing line is strong, invisible and holds varying weights.
2. *Damage* to walls and woodwork should not occur because of nails or other suporting devices, and permission *must always* be obtained before any nails are hammered into the fabric of the church.
3. *Moisture* should be provided for fresh plant material but no damage by water should be caused to the fabric of the church. The use of polythene prevents this and also holds in moisture for the plant material. Protective polythene sheeting should be used while working.
4. *Unusual placements* for decorations should not be used without permission because flowers must never impede the movements of the clergy or the congregation.

12

Large Size Flower Arrangements

Larger than normal flower arrangements are sometimes needed for greater impact. They can be made for special events such as harvest and flower festivals, Christmas services and weddings, and can be seen easily by everyone even when the church is packed with people. One extra large arrangement is usually far more effective than numerous small ones that can give an over-decorated, fussy appearance to a church. Larger designs are necessary in a cathedral because smaller arrangements look insignificant in the vast spaces under the lofty roofs.

There are various ways of making big arrangements and none is difficult once you know how to construct them. Whatever method is used the chief problem is stability. You must be quite certain that an arrangement cannot fall over. *The taller the design the more top-heavy it can become*, especially if containers filled with water or foam are used well above ground level. A heavy base, or weights such as stones, bricks or sand added to the lowest container, is usually the answer and the taller the design the heavier must be the base to prevent it from falling over.

Most flower arrangers feel happier if they are able to wire a big arrangement to a permanent feature in the church such as a pillar or built-in screen. This also prevents it from falling over if accidentally knocked.

Simple large arrangements

The simplest method of achieving a large design is to use a very big container such as a heavy garden urn and arrange plant material in it that is large in size, and has long stems. It is not necessary to have a great many flowers and leaves to make an arrangement big and often the most beautiful are made with a minimum of plant material. Ideal are hydrangeas, the larger varieties of dahlias and chrysanthemums, tall delphiniums and eremurus, long branches of fruit blossom and lime flowers, enormous branches of evergreens, the biggest hosta and artichoke leaves. Choose the largest plant material you can find.

A pedestal made of marble, alabaster, wrought iron, wood or stone is excellent for lifting an arrangement to give greater height. A baking tin container will hold the plant material.

A five feet high arrangement of hosta leaves and dahlias in a garden urn

Another simple way of making an outsize flower arrangement is to use two containers, one tall and one flat. There should be enough space in the chosen position for the tall container to be placed behind the lower one. Put foam in both and then add plant material so that the design appears integrated, as one arrangement. The lower container may be visible but the flowers and leaves placed in it hide the taller container. No tubes or cones should be necessary for added height but they could be used if desired.

Designs can also be constructed without visible containers and many ingenious mechanics have been evolved to hold plant material in water

A simple tall arrangement

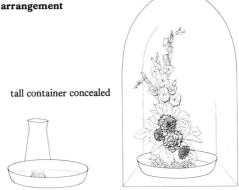

tall container concealed

or foam many feet from ground level. They can give a dramatic and lovely effect and can be seen from far away.

Placing flowers in containers above your normal reach is not always easy and a stepladder is essential. Getting up and down the ladder to judge the effect each time you add a flower stem is a tiring job. A trusted mate can be a great help to direct operations from floor level. Sometimes it is possible to place the top flowers and leaves in the design before lifting the construction into position.

There are several types of support that can be inexpensively constructed and also several ways of making bases heavy and stable. Variations of these can be made to suit individual requirements.

CONSTRUCTION 1 A tall column

Obtain a wooden stake not less than 2 inches square and of the required length. Paint it dark green, brown or black. This can be made into a useful stand for mounting metal cones to hold water or foam, and plant material. Attach the cones to the stake by winding insulating tape around each cone and the stake. For extra security, instead of tape, use heavy wire which can be stapled on to the stake. The cones should be placed at intervals on both sides and in the centre of the stake. The flowers placed in one cone will hide the cone above.

It is not necessary to place cones at the bottom of the stake. Here an arrangement in a normal container can be placed which adds weight to the base.

This type of basic construction gives a rather slim design when finished.

THE BASE. The bottom of the stake may be held in position in one of the

138

following ways:

1. It may be screwed to a wooden block using angle irons or brackets.
2. It may be placed in a metal holder that is screwed down to a block of wood.
3. It may be pushed into a plastic bucket or large, empty paint can containing plaster of Paris.

Construction 1

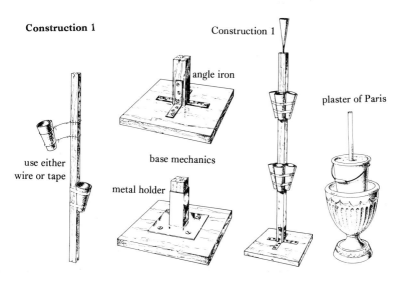

Construction 1

angle iron

plaster of Paris

use either
wire or tape

base mechanics

metal holder

Plaster of Paris is obtainable as a white powder from a chemist. Fill the bucket with the powder and gradually stir in cold water. Do not use a pottery container, or one that will break easily, as it will crack at this stage of the operation. Have everything ready as the plaster sets in a few minutes. As soon as it is like thick, whipped cream put in the end of the stake making sure that it is upright and in the correct position. Hold it for a few minutes, after which time the stake should stand alone. A few heavy stones may be placed in the bottom of the bucket to give extra weight. Cement or concrete (cement with added sand and gravel) may be used instead of plaster of Paris, and are obtainable from builders merchants but they set slowly and the stake must have temporary support. The bucket may be placed into an outer, decorative container such as a garden urn. Make sure that the bucket fits before you start and add bricks, stones, gravel or sand to the outer container to give extra bottom weight. Alternatively the bucket can be concealed by plant material arranged in a container in front.

For a column 8 feet 6 inches tall:

stake 2 inches square, 5 feet long, painted, mat dark green or black;

base 15 inches square, $\frac{3}{4}$ inch wood, painted;

7 metal cones, $2\frac{1}{2}$-inch diameter, about $9\frac{1}{2}$ inches long;

4 angle irons;

Screw the stake towards the back of the base using the angle irons; then wire one cone to the top of the stake, and three cones 9 inches below the top, one in the middle and two on either side. Three more cones should be wired 9 inches below the bottom of the upper three cones. Then place a container, such as a loaf tin, at the bottom of the stake on the base. This may be made into an all round design by placing two more cones at the back with the groups of three. The stake should be screwed to the middle of the base, and loaf tins placed at the bottom on either side.

CONSTRUCTION 2 A wide cone

A wider design in a cone shape can be made by surrounding a similar stake with crumpled wire netting secured with reel wire to nails placed in the stake at intervals. The wire netting can be filled with long-lasting evergreens and cones on sticks can be inserted into the wire netting to hold water for flowers. Bunches of grapes may be wired to the netting.

CONSTRUCTION 3 A slim column

Using reel wire, bind a stake with a thick layer of damp sphagnum moss. This can be bought from a florist. The easiest way to do this is to spread the moss on newspaper and lay the stake on top of it. Hammer a nail into the top of the stake and twist on to it the end of a reel of wire. Push the moss around the stake and at the same time encircle it with reel wire in

Construction 2 and 3

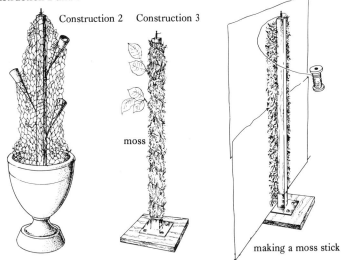

Construction 2   Construction 3

moss

making a moss stick

140

two-inch loops. When you reach the bottom twist it round several times and then loop the wire back again to the top of the stake.

Sprigs of woody stemmed foliage can easily be pushed into the moss and fruit can be held in place if impaled on to skewers or short lengths of narrow dowel. Flowers can also be inserted into the moss if they have strong stems and if the moss is not too tightly packed. The bottom of the stake may be supported as before. This makes a slim design.

CONSTRUCTION 4 A slim column

A similar decoration up to 5 feet tall can be made using a flower arranger's metal drape stand. Extend the stand almost as far as it will

Construction 4

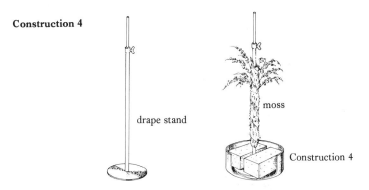

drape stand

moss

Construction 4

stretch and then tighten the screw, wiring it so that it cannot slip, before covering it with moss as above. A drape stand has its own welded base and it will stay in position if a heavy container is placed on top of it, or if the base is secured with plasticine or a similar compound to a shallow container such as a cake tin. Place soaked foam on top of the base to hold it down firmly in the container. This makes an attractive decoration for the end of a pew or choir stall. A similar but wider and fuller design can be made by threading blocks of foam on to a broom stick screwed to a wooden base and placed in a cake tin. Wrap the foam in polythene to conserve moisture and then in wire netting if desired. It is essential to use a container at the bottom to catch dripping water. This can also be made into a design to be seen all round.

CONSTRUCTION 5 A huge pyramid

An even bigger pyramid can be made 10 or more feet tall using a central stake of wood as the backbone. Attach the stake to a circular wooden base and place this in a round, plastic washing-up bowl. Fill the bowl with blocks of foam standing upright and fill in any spaces with further pieces. Wind a length of wire netting the same height as the stake around the foam and wire the cut ends together to form a tube. Add

141

Construction 5, 6

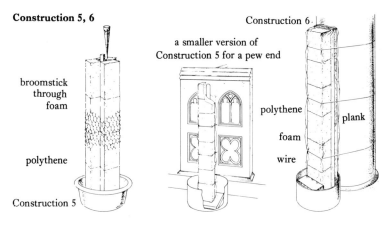

Construction 6

a smaller version of
Construction 5 for a pew end

broomstick
through
foam

polythene

foam

wire

plank

polythene

Construction 5

further blocks standing one on top of another all the way up and around the stake. Pull the wire netting tightly around the foam to hold it in position, so that you end up with a cone of netting encircling the foam around a strong central column. This construction will hold a large quantity of flowers and leaves in an all-round design and provide them with ample water. A further 3 to 4 feet can be added at the top by placing tall stems, and cones holding plant material, in the top blocks of foam. A dramatic effect is obtained by massing only one variety of flower such as gladioli and this is a good decoration on top of a font.

CONSTRUCTION 6 A tall design against a pillar or screen

Obtain a wooden plank 4 inches wide and of the required length. Knock long nails through it at 3 inch intervals. Spread a length of thin polythene on the floor and place the plank on top if it. Impale blocks of foam on the nails all along the stake. Wrap the polythene around the foam, securing it with sticky tape at intervals and, if the plank is exceptionally long, wrap wire netting around it for extra security. When securely wrapped, lift the stake into position, placing the bottom of the plank into a container that will catch any water leaking down.

To hold the plank in position against a pillar or screen, carry strong wires around the decoration and the pillar in at least three places. Make sure the pillar or screen is strong enough to support the weight. There is no need for weight at the base as the construction is held firmly against the pillar. A large amount of plant material can be used in this type of construction.

CONSTRUCTION 7 A series of vertical triangles

Obtain a wooden stake 2 inches square and of the required height. Attach two or more shelves to this, one at the top and the others about 3—4 feet apart down the stake, holding them by brackets. In between the

142

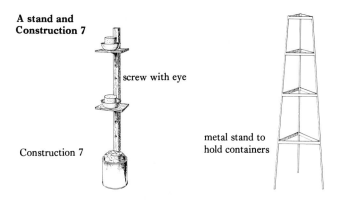

A stand and Construction 7

screw with eye

Construction 7

metal stand to hold containers

shelves add screws with eyes. Attach wire to these for wrapping around a pillar or other permanent architectural feature. The base can be supported as described earlier. The shelves can each hold a container filled with foam and wire netting but these must be firmly held in place by attaching wire to the netting and then carrying it around the stake.

This construction can hold a large quantity of plant material in a design that looks like a series of triangles one on top of the other.

Concealing mechanics

Basic mechanics can be concealed by placing plant material over them, the flowers and leaves in one container hiding the container above. When making a tall column with moss or foam and without cones, it is best to cover the mechanics with leaves placed flat against the column inserted into the moss or foam before adding fruit or flowers. It is easier to insert stems of foliage at this stage and also more economical because fewer flowers and fruit are needed. It is a waste to use expensive flowers to hide mechanics. This can be done so much better with leaves that also provide a good plain background for colourful flowers or fruit. Easily obtainable longlasting foliage such as box, cupressus, yew, beech and laurel is ideal. Hard or woody stems are essential as soft stems are tedious to insert. They break or bend and usually need a hole to be made before they can be inserted. If no suitable foliage is available in local gardens it can usually be found in flower markets or a florist can obtain it.

Plinths

A plinth made of wood is excellent for lifting any design. It is especially useful for a Cathedral flower festival to raise an arrangement so that it can be seen above the heads of people. Paint the plinth in a dull colour, or fabric or Fablon may be used to cover the wood. Large plinths should

143

be professionally made as they may need support in the centre to hold the weight of the construction on top.

A twenty feet column in green and white flowers and foliage, in four containers wired wigwam fashion to rods cemented into the base, arranged by the York Flower Club in York Minster. By courtesy of Graham Powell

144

13

Earlier Customs with Flowers

I cannot help wondering, when I see flowers lovingly arranged nowadays in our old churches, how the custom of bringing flowers, leaves and fruit into the church originated. Who arranged the flowers and what form did the decorations take? It is not easy to find references to the use of flowers in worship in earlier days but, thanks to the diligence of churchwardens, monks and other men of religion in keeping records we can find out more about the times after the Middle Ages.

Early Flower Decoration

Floral decoration is as old as civilization itself. For centuries flowers have been cut and placed in vases of water and they have been a continual inspiration for the adornment of architecture, furnishings and utensils.

There is ample evidence, in wall paintings and bas-relief in Egyptian tombs, to show that the ancient Egyptians used cut flowers in vases and when Howard Carter discovered Tutankhamen's tomb he found many wreaths and three huge necklaces of flowers; garlands of leaves; one hundred and sixteen baskets of dried fruits and seeds; elaborate bouquets; simple bunches of flowers and on the forehead of the young King a simple circlet of spring flowers.

Grains, fruit and flowers in baskets were presented as ceremonial offerings by the ancient Greeks, so that the chief use of plant material was symbolic rather than decorative. Gifts for gods or men were often wreaths, garlands, bouquets, or flower heads piled in baskets or laid out on trays. Garland-making was a profession in ancient Greece and Darius the Great is said to have employed forty-six garland makers in his household.

The ancient Indian offering to Buddha, a narrow-necked bowl of full-blown lotuses and buds, was also symbolic. The lotus symbolised the universe and the bowl held 'the water of life'. This custom of the lotus offering travelled with the Buddhist religion to China and Japan and in China blossoms in vases have been set upon the altars since the beginning of the T'ang dynasty (618–906 AD), by which time Buddhism was widely accepted.

Throughout history, and in all parts of the world, flowers have been carried to temples and churches, offered to the gods and placed on the tombs of martyrs as symbols of man's need or appreciation and as a sign of worship of God, the gods or saintly men. It is said of the early churches that around the altar there was a perpetual harvest festival scene, an expression of that primitive instinct in man that he should not approach his god empty-handed.

The Early Church

It was an early pagan practice to garland sepulchres with flowers. The early Christians however were not conformists and refused to copy this custom. Jesus' love of nature is apparent in his parables. 'Consider the lilies of the field, how they grow; they toil not, neither do they spin: yet I say unto you, that even Solomon in all his glory was not arrayed like one of these.' (Matthew 6 v. 28)

In the second century, Minucius Felix wrote 'Who is he who doubts of our indulging ourselves in spring flowers, when we gather both the rose of spring and the lily, and whatever else is of agreeable colour and odour among the flowers? For these we both use scattered loose and free, and we twine our necks with them in garlands. Please excuse us for not crowning our heads: we are accustomed to receive the scent of a sweet flower in our nostrils, not to inhale it with the back of our heads or our hair. Nor do we crown the dead. And in this respect I the more wonder at you, in the way in which you apply to a lifeless person, or to one who does not feel, a torch, or a garland to one who does not smell it. ... We adorn our obsequies with the same tranquillity with which we live; and we do not bind to us a withering garland, but we wear one living with eternal flowers from God, since we, being most moderate and secure in the liberality of our God, are animated by the hope of future bliss by confidence in his present sovereignty'.

Although the early Christians did not 'crown the dead' they saw a relationship between flowers and death and felt that the flowers were symbolic of the garden of paradise which lay beyond the grave. The North African martyr, Perpetua, referred to her after life in 'a vast space like a pleasure-garden, having rose trees and every kind of flower'. This association of flowers, paradise and martyrdom led to the floral decoration of the tombs of saints and eventually to the more general use of flowers upon the graves of Christians.

It is not clear how flowers began to be part of normal worship in church. One theory is that it stemmed from the practice of placing flowers on and near a martyr's tomb. From the fourth century in the

West an altar became connected with the devotion to a martyr and was located above the burial place. After some time a church was often built around the tomb and so the flowers that continued to be brought to the martyr gradually became associated with the surrounding church. The form of the floral tribute is not clear but in c. 535–c. 600 Venantius Fortunatus wrote.

'When winter holds the world in its icy clasp, flowers, which are the ornaments of the fields, fall and perish. In the spring, when our Lord conquered hell, the grass rises again joyfully and covers the earth with abundant tresses. Here men decorate the doors and pulpits with flowers; there they fill the folds of their tunics with perfumed roses; you gather them only for Christ, perfumes, pious first fruits which you bear to church. You arrange diverse wreaths for the fortunate altars. Beneath these flowers the altar seems brilliant with embroidery; golden saffron units with violet; white and purple shimmer here and the azure is mingled with the green. The flowers rival each other in their colours and seem to give themselves to a unique combat within this haven of peace. This one gives pleasure by its brilliant whiteness, that one by its admirable redness; this one is more scented, that one owes its beauty to its scarlet hue. So the flowers strive with each other and their scent is better than incense.'

Nowhere is it written that flowers were actually arranged on the altar, but from this quotation it seems that they were suspended above it, probably in the form of garlands or wreaths. Gregory of Tours (538–594) a historian and ecclesiastic wrote about the walls as the main areas of decoration.

According to a French writer of the seventeenth century, in a treatise on altars, there was no mention of altar flowers during the first twelve centuries and in 1688 he records that flowers 'are still not placed on the altars of Cathedrals were care has been taken to retain the ancient customs'.

The Fifth Century to the Sixteenth Century

The Middle Ages are considered by historians to be from the fifth century up to the latter part of the fifteenth century. The Reformation started in Germany at the beginning of the sixteenth century and spread rapidly over Europe. The adoption of the book of Common Prayer came in England in 1549.

It has been said that 'over the whole medieval world lay the broad shadow of the Cross'. The church at that time was not only the House of God but the meeting hall and theatre, the centre of all community life.

Church festivals were a major event in people's lives and were preceded by processions when flowers were strewn along the roads to churches. Flower garlands were used to decorate the crosses and the huge tapers that were carried in the processions. Both crosses, tapers and garlands were then transferred to the church on arrival.

We have information about the flowers used in worship during the later years of this period because of the careful records kept by the churchwardens, especially the accounts that showed full details of every item used in the services of the church. Flowers were still not used on the altar, as far as we know. The following representative selection of entries is fascinating.

St Mary-at-Hill, London

1483	For garlandes on Corpus Christi Day		
	Woodruff for St. Barnabas Day		$8\frac{1}{2}$d
1487–8	Paid for holm and ivy against Christmas		1d
1490–1	For palms, cakes and flowers for Palm		
	Sunday		7d
1526–7	Paid for garlands and roses and lavender		
	on Corpus Christi Day	2s	5d
1539–40	Paid for palm, box and ivy and		
	flowers and cakes		17d

St Margarets, Westminster

1544	Paid for rushes against the Dedication		
	Day which is always the first Sunday		
	of October	1s	5d
1647	Paid for rosemaries and bays, that was		
	stuck about the church at Christmas	1s	6d

Other records provide the same picture. Spenser in 1579 writes

'Youths now flock in everywhere
To gather May buskets and smelling briar,
And home they hasten the posts to dight,
And all the Church pillars ere daylight'.

John Stow, in his Survey of London published in 1603, tells how 'against the feast of Christmas, every man's house, as also their parish churches, were decked with holme, Ivy, Bays, and whatsoever the season of the year afforded to be green'.

Country churches show few records that refer to flowers because these were given by local people and greenery could be collected from the countryside.

We can conclude from writings that floral decoration of churches in the Middle Ages and up to the end of the Stuart period in the early eighteenth century was confined to major festivals and was not a weekly practice for the normal church services.

The festivals were associated with traditional shrubs and greenery. Sweet smelling herbs, especially rosemary and fennel, were used in abundance and the floors were covered with rushes. Green garlands were hung from roofs, walls and pillars, but on Corpus Christi day in accordance with traditional practice, red roses were used for the garlands and Stow writes that in the procession at St. Paul's, on the Feast of the Apostle, 'the Dean and Chapter apparalled in coats and vestments with garlands of roses on their heads issued out of the West door'.

It appears that rushes and herbs were also used to strew the floors when distinguished visitors were expected.

St Martins in the Field, 1571

'For Rishes and strawing herbs when the bishoppe came in visitacion to ye church—XIJd

Stow also writes 'on the Vigil of St. John the Baptist and S. S. Peter and Paul every man's door in London was shadowed with green birch, long fennel, St. Johns wort, orpin, white lilies and such like, garnished upon with beautiful flowers'. Many of these customs survived until the eighteenth century.

Flowers and greenery

Although flowers are mentioned it seems that greenery was used far more often. This is probably because flowers were in short supply. Flower gardens were not plentiful and usually the flowers grew wild. The Romans were gardeners and grew rosa gallica, lavender and mint with which to make toilet waters but even their gardens consisted mostly of lawns and shrubs, fountains and topiary. After the fall of the Roman Empire in the fifth century gardening lapsed into a decline.

Eventually during medieval times small walled gardens were established and the monks were well known for the gardens they cultivated behind their monastery walls. We might well call them kitchen gardens because their main purpose was to produce herbs for making medicine, salads or 'sallets' and flavourings for food. Many herbs and a few simple flowers such as marigolds, violets, roses, irises and primroses, were grown for their medicinal uses, although roses and lilies were grown for ornament from early times. The exquisite illuminated manuscripts of the time show the flowers.

The real development of gardens both for pleasure and for medicinal and culinary purposes came in the fifteenth and sixteenth centuries when it was no longer necessary to live behind walls for protection. The abbey churches had especially good gardens because it was the sacristans duty to provide flowers for the church festivals.

In 1597 John Gerard's Herball was first published in London and in 1629 *Paradisi In Sole Paradisus Terrestris* by John Parkinson (A Garden of all sorts of pleasant flowers which our Englise ayre will permitt to be noursed up . . .'. Both men were physicians, botanists and owners of fine gardens and their books did much to interest people in flowers. The first botanical garden was made in Oxford in 1632 but a more advanced knowledge of gardening practices had been brought to England by Protestant Flemish Refugees escaping from the Spaniards in the time of Elizabeth the First (1558–1603).

Fragrance

For many years it was considered essential to grow fragrant herbs and flowers because it was thought that their perfume could clear the air of pestilence. Rushes were strewn on the floors of houses and churches to clean them and make them habitable. A few sweet smelling clippings were added to the straws. In 1560 a Dutch physician Levinus Lenious visited England and afterwards wrote of the English

'Their chambers and parlours strewed over with sweet herbs refreshed mee; their nosegays finely intermingled with sundry sorts of fragraunte flowers, in their bedchambers and privy rooms, with comfortable smell cheered me up and entirely delyghted all my senses—altho we do trimme up our parlours with green boughes freshe herbs or vine leaves no nation does it more decently more trimmely nor more sightly than they doe in England'

Fragrance was also necessary because of the badly drained streets and lack of sanitation and damp courses. These conditions, which continued until the end of the eighteenth century. Apart from this it was the perpetuation of a custom to strew the floor at important religious festivals.

Germander (Teucrium, a shrub) and hyssop (a bitter, minty herb) were the most common plants used. Rushes were used where there was wealth. 'Rushes' were the stems of Sweet Flag (Acorus salamus, with a refreshing lemon smell) and these only grew in the fenlands of Norfolk,

Cambridgeshire and low-lying areas of Europe and so obtaining them could be expensive. Amongst twenty plants recommended later for strewing by Thomas Tusser of Essex in his One Hundred Points of Good Husbandry published in 1557 were basil and balm; camomile and costmery; Lavendar and hyssop, sage and thyme. Meadowsweet was popular with Elizabeth the First and rue was in demand since it kept away fleas. The perfume of these plants was released as they were trodden on.

On special occasions fragrant plants played an important part in the ceremony

1065, on December 28th, Edward the Confessor's first abbey of Westminster was consecrated and it is recorded that hyssop was strewn over the floor

1162, when Thomas Becket was made Archbishop of Canterbury he ordered his hall to be strewn each day in spring with fresh May blossoms; in the summer with sweet scented rushes '. . . that such knights as the benches could not contain might sit on the floor without dirtying their clothes'

1299, on January 6th, King Edward I offered frankincense and myrrh in his Chapel Royal

1495 Roger de Walden was made Bishop of St Pauls and was crowned with a garland of scented red roses

1437 at the time of the accession of James II Mary Vowle was appointed 'strewer of Herbs in Ordinary to His Majesty' and before the coronation ceremony in Westminster Abbey she received instructions from the Lord Almoner to spread two breadths of blue broadcloth from the stone steps in the hall to the foot of the steps in the choir 'which cloth is to be strewn with nine baskets full of sweet herbs and flowers'. (For more about the scents and smells of Early England read A History of Scent by Roy Genders)

Symbolism

The symbolism of flowers during medieval times remained up to the late sixteenth century. It could be interesting to refer to this in present day church festivals. Symbolism was long established and was a mixture of classical, pagan, Christian, secular and religious beliefs and associations. The meaning of a flower varied sometimes from country to country and from age to age but was of great importance as a means of giving messages to people, a large number of whom could not read. Plants, colours and even numbers were significant in paintings and other works of art, especially those with religious subjects. I feel it is logical to assume that at times when flowers were placed in the lower part of the church (below the Sanctuary) they could have been chosen, to convey similar meanings to the flowers shown in paintings.

It is difficult to be accurate about the early spiritual meanings of flowers because legend and fact have become intertwined but many of the legends attached to flowers have a logical explanation. For example it seems natural to have chosen the daisy as a symbol of innocence and the violet for humility.

One can assume fairly safely that the following associations were used in Gothic times (1200–1425) when symbolism was of great importance.

balsam	consolation
borage	courage
cedar	steadfastness
columbine	the Virgin's woe
crocus	joy
cyclamen	passion of Christ
fig	fidelity; argumentativeness
fruit	achievement, apple—man's fall
grain	bread of the Sacrament
grapevine	Christ and his disciples
laurel	peace (also sweet bay)
lily	purity, fertility, the Virgin's flower
oak	strength
rose	divine love, the Virigin's flower; if red, the flower of martyrs; symbol of silence
plantain	the road to Christ
rosemary	remembrance
sweet woodruff	found in the straw of the Virgin's bed at the birth of Christ and called Lady's (our Lady's) bedstraw
violet	humility

Colour associations in ritual

black	sorrow
blue	faith, fidelity, the Virgin's colour
golden yellow	light, joy, the colour of heaven
green	hope, eternal life
red	sacrifice, suffering, martyrdom
violet	meditation
white	purity

152

A study of Renaissance paintings is interesting because the painters of religious subjects included flowers long associated with Christian legend. Florentine artists such as Botticelli, Leonardo da Vinci and Raphael chose the plant material that they included in their paintings with much care and erudition, and their work influenced other artists. Raphael in his 'Alba Madonna', included anemones, cyclamen, dandelions, Epimedium alpinum, bedstraw, plantain, sorrel and violets, which translated meant Mary, image of humility (violet) on her bed of straw bore Him who led us out of the barren pagan world (epimedium alpinum). All men find their way to Him (plantain). He suffered death (anemone); bitter was the Virgin's sorrow (cyclamen, dandelion, sorrel).

Some Renaissance meanings are

anenome	the 'Easter flower'; Christ's blood fell on it at Calvary; its trilobed leaf was symbolic of the Trinity in the early Christian church
cyclamen	(white) the 'bleeding nun', symbol of sorrow because of its red centre
dandelion	bitter herb of the Passion
epimedium alpinum	associated with barren soil
forget-me-not or scorpion grass	good for scorpion bite; the Virgin's flower because she trod on the scorpion or serpent, Satan
iris	the passion of Christ
rose	Venus; the Virgin; love; silence
sorrel	bitter herb of the Passion; because of its arrow-shaped leaf it was also associated with the plague which struck like an arrow

A useful book to study on the floral symbols of the Renaissance is 'Signs and Symbols in Christian Art' by George Ferguson, 1961.

The Virgin's flowers

rose	she was the rose of Sharon
lily	her chastity; her purity
voilet, daisy and other 'shy' flowers	her humility
columbine, foxglove and campanula	the Gloves of Mary
pink	the herb of the Virgin

The lilium candidum appeared so often in paintings of the Annunciation that it was soon called the Madonna lily. Before the lily was introduced into northern Europe, the iris was used by Flemish artists as the Virgin's flower. It is often seen placed in the hands of the Archangel Gabriel or set in a vase by the Virgin's side. In Roman Catholic countries the snowdrop was dedicated to the Virgin.

Other legendary associations are

acacia	immortality of the soul
almond	divine approval or favor
apple	salvation was shown in the hands of Jesus Christ or the Virgin, sin when shown in the hands of Adam. Three apples a symbol of St Dorothea
briar	grief and tribulation
bulrush	hope of salvation to the faithful
carnation	the Incarnation of Christ; helpful against the plague
cherry	the symbol of good works
Christmas rose	the nativity
clover	the Trinity because of its leaf
columbine	the seven gifts of the Holy Spirit with which the Christ Child was endowed at birth because of its seven petals. Seven blooms were sometimes shown in paintings for the same reason
cypress	death
daisy	innocence
grape and vine	associated with the Eucharist
holly	grief and tribulation
hyacinth	heaven
ivy	life eternal and fidelity because of the colour and clinging habit
jasmine	chastity
laurel	triumph. Suggestive of eternity because the foliage wilts slowly
lily, orange	a royal symbol and signifying the Christ Child as King of Heaven; the Passion of Christ
lily of the valley	purity; humility
narcissus	the triumph of Divine love
oak	faith and endurance
olive branch	peace

palm	the palm of the Roman victory became the sign of the martyr in his victory over death
pansy	the three coloured petals represented the Trinity. Sometimes known as the Trinity herb
pomegranate	fertility; because of the unity of many seeds in one fruit it is also said to resemble the church
rose	the attribute of Venus goddess of love became a symbol of pure love and sacrifice
strawberry flower and fruit	the fruits of the Spirit or the rewards that were bestowed on the righteous believer for his good deeds; righteousness
thistle	earthly sorrow and tribulation
wheat	associated with the Eucharist when with grapes or vine and a single ear a symbol of the Resurrection, a seed to fall and be reborn in a new life; bountifulness; a sheaf is thanksgiving

The Seventeenth to the Twentieth Centuries

George Herbertin 'Priest to the Temple' mentions that amongst the duties of the wardens in the Seventeenth century was to 'keep the church clean without dust or cobwebs and that at festivals, it must be strewed and stuck with boughs and perfumed with incense'. On such occasions when it was usual for the lord of the manor his lady and other members of his household to attend, the stone floor was covered with fragrant rushes and leaves

> Thou knave but for thee 'are this time of day
> My lady's fair pew had been strewed full gay
> With primroses, cowslips and violets sweet
> With mints and marigold, and marjoram meet
>
> (from Apius and Virginia)

Flowers came into vogue more universally after the middle of the seventeenth century as foreign plants in increasing numbers reached England. However the puritanical reforms of Cromwell during 1649 to 1660 did not encourage a time of joy in flowers or even boughs of greenery. Many statues and stained glass windows were destroyed at this time and the Cromwellians attempted to suppress Christmas but they introduced new, commemoration days of their own and flowers and herbs were still used in these services.

'For hearbes and lawrell strewed in the church on October 24th (Thanksgiving Day for victory at Worcester) . . . 8.0'

The Gentleman's Magazine in July 1783 referred to 'the flowers with which many of our churches are ornamented on Easter Day'. Pinks, Polyanthus, Sweet William, Gilliflowers, Carnations, Mignionettes, Thyme, Hyssop, Camomile and Rosemary' are mentioned in 1804.

At the opening of the nineteenth century and in the early part of Queen Victoria's reign the condition of churches is said to have been disgraceful. Many chancels were used as schools, much stained glass was destroyed. This followed the eighteenth century social and political upheavals arising from the French revolution and the Industrial revolution. Poverty was rife and there was little money to spare for the church. In 1840 a body of reformers, known as The Ecclesiologists, did much to restore mutilated and neglected churches and to renew pride in the church surroundings. They were not happy about flowers on altars but were enthusiastic about floral decoration in the rest of the church. In their journal, The Ecclesiologist, in 1846 there is an article with the title 'On Flowers as Employed in the Adornment of Churches'. This advocated the use of more colour and encourages the use of flowers 'because our country cannot find the rich marbles which glorify the churches of the south'. A book written by Henry L. Jenner in 1847 used the same title and in 1868 Edward Young Cox wrote a book called 'The Art of Garnishing Churches at Christmas time and Other Festivals'. This was so popular that three editions were printed within three years. In 1882 Ernest Geldart published The Art of Garnishing Churches.

The fact that such books were published shows that there must have been a great deal of interest in church decoration. This reflected the general popularity of flowers, and their arrangement, in Victorian times. Many a young girl had to spend at least half an hour every morning 'doing the flowers'. Many upper class homes had conservatories and there was a great revival of gardens. Fascination with all types of floral decoration abounded and flowers were made of shells, wool, wax, feathers, leather, seeds and even hair. Fashioning a nosegay or 'tussy-mussy' was another accomplishment and no well dressed lady appeared at a social gathering without one. The entire nineteenth century was one of great enthusiasm for plants, gardening and flowers in every form. There were many new introductions from abroad, and people also became avid collectors. It is small wonder that churches as well as homes began to be over-decorated.

In 1868 the choir of St Pauls was decorated for Christmas, for the first time, with hot house plants and by 1970 many churches were described as 'Choral and Floral'. Victorian ladies had plenty of leisure and designs for churches became as ornate as Victorian homes. Cardboard banners, showing texts, were sold for use in churches and these had holes for the insertion of holly and evergreens. Artificial reredos', constructed from lathes and wire, were hung with holly, stars and crosses. Often every corner, column and arch was smothered in greenery, hiding much of the beautiful fabric of the church building

Eventually special flower services were instituted. At St James Aldgate, Mitre Square, a special flower sermon was preached every Whit Tuesday evening. We are told that the church was decked with flowers, the congregation carried nosegays, and a bouquet was placed on the pulpit. In 1866 the text for the sermon was 'Let the earth bring forth grasses', Genesis i.11, and the preacher stressed that a blade of grass could teach us much. How full of testimony it was to the goodness of the Creator who has covered the earth with this enamelled carpet of soft fragrant verdure to refresh and gladden our hearts'.

The diary of Parson Kilvert describes a harvest festival in 1870 'Cooper came down with his men carrying magnificent ferns and plants and began to work in the chancel. One fine silver fern was put in the font. Gibbins undertook the font and dressed it very tastefully with moss and white asters under the sweeping fronds of the silver fern. Round the stem were twined the delicate light green sprays of white convolvulus. The pillars were wreathed and twined with wild hop vine falling in graceful, careless festoons and curling tendrils from wreath and capital'.

Ernest Geldart eventually condemned the way in which a sanctuary may be 'perverted into a horticultural show' because the Victorians often obscured the building, erected complicated trellises, displayed emblematic devices and mottoes, and misused the church furniture. Geldart sensibly wrote 'Clearly there is a fitness in the use of as much white as possible on white days and of red at Pentecost, and of blue and white on feasts of the virgin; but to say that blue is unfit for Easter, or red or yellow, or indeed any colour, is to go beyond all reason and sense'.

Meanwhile what of flower arrangements on the altar? The ancient custom was that nothing should stand upon the table except what was needed for the celebration of the Lord's Supper, and the first reference to vases is found in 1606 in a Caerimoniale Episcoporum published in Rome. When the practice of placing objects other than the eucharist vessels began, this opened the way for flowers and in time this became general in the Roman Catholic Church. Thiers in 1688 wrote 'Flowers, either natural or artificial, are today the usual ornament of the majority of altars. They are decorated with them at all seasons'. In 1823 an account of Christmas festivities reads that 'the altars were with flowers, and the churches profusely decorated'. The Protestant church did not adopt this fashion as quickly and Peter Anson in 'Fashions in Church Furnishing, 1840–1940', writes that by 1850 'vases of flowers had not yet become popular' but Pugin in his study of The Present State of Ecclesiastical Architecture in England, 1843 wrote

'before the twelfth century flowers were not suffered on altars although the custom of hanging garlands and branches on great feasts, to decorate the church, is of the highest antiquity: even the whole pavement was not unfrequently sprinkled with flowers and aromatic herbs but', he continued 'every reflecting mind must be both struck and pained with incongruous decorations of most of the modern altars; the chief aim of those who arrange them appears to be merely a great show. All mystical reasons, all ancient discipline, all dignity and solemnity are utterly lost sight of; everything is overdone. Candlesticks are piled on candlesticks as if arranged for sale; whole rows of flower pots mingled with reliquaries, images and not unfrequently profane ornaments; festoons of upholsterer's drapery; even distorting and distracting looking glasses are introduced into this medley display; the effect of which upon persons who are conversant with ancient discipline and practice it is not easy to describe'.

However Roman Catholic churches and chapels continued to have altar flowers and the Church of England eventually followed this custom. Arguments about whether they should be used continued until they reached a climax in 1870 with the case of Elphinstone v Purches, when the verdict of the Court of Arches was that the placing of vases upon the altar was 'an innocuous and not unseemly decoration'. From then onwards flowers have been arranged on the altar in most Anglican churches. Many of the present day altar vases are copies of Gothic or Renaissance ecclesiastical containers.

As the enthusiasm for over-decorative effects faded in the Victorian age, the first years of the twentieth century led to the use of altar flowers only for daily services. Only the best flowers were used and although the arrangements may not have been artistic the blooms were certainly perfect.

In 1920 Hewlett Johnson, Dean of Manchester wrote in favour of more colour in the church, 'Flowers should stand in glass vases on the altar and in great bowls on the floor beside it or on a low stand by the chancel steps. And there should be flowers in the porch to welcome me'.

After the Second World War many flower arrangement clubs were founded leading to the formation of the National Association of Flower Arrangement Societies of Great Britain and with this came an enlightened approach to the arrangement of flowers in churches. There has been a growing appreciation of the work of the church flower arrangers who with dedicated skill seek to enhance the beauty of the stonework and of the church furnishings. Their aim is to complement and not hide the treasures of the church so that there is a sense of harmony and beauty. Many people regard arranging the flowers in the church as an act of devotion in itself and seek to improve their skill and knowledge. Sometimes special flower festivals are held and many thousands of flower club members and church flower arrangers give happily of their time and their flowers to make churches even more beautiful. All over the British Isles these festivals have been, and continue to be, held in tiny village churches and in great Cathedrals. Many thousands of pounds have been raised by opening the festivals to the admiring and incredulous public. This has enabled urgent repairs and maintenance to be undertaken; has brought a communal spirit amongst the flower arrangers and the parish; has interested many people in visiting churches that otherwise they would never have seen; made possible the purchase of new church furnishings, but above all shown to the world the loveliness of God's creations in the beauty of a church setting and in the words of Van Ogden Vogt, 'the experience of faith and the experience of beauty are in some measure identical'.

'The Amen of nature is always a flower'

Oliver Wendell Holmes